Navigating Autism: A Parent's Guide To Understanding And Supporting Their Child

Barley Nicola

Published by Barley Nicola, 2024.

NAVIGATING AUTISM: A PARENT'S GUIDE TO UNDERSTANDING AND SUPPORTING THEIR CHILD

First edition. March 30, 2024.

Copyright © 2024 Barley Nicola.

ISBN: 979-8224817016

Written by Barley Nicola.

Table of Contents

Chapter 1: Introduction

- UNDERSTANDING AUTISM Spectrum disorder

Autism Spectrum Disorder (ASD) is a complex neurodevelopmental disorder that affects individuals in various ways. It is characterized by difficulties in social communication and interactions, as well as repetitive behaviors and restricted interests. ASD is often diagnosed in early childhood, although some individuals may not receive a diagnosis until later in life. The symptoms of ASD can range from mild to severe, and no two individuals with ASD are exactly alike.

One of the key features of ASD is the difficulty in understanding and interpreting social cues. Individuals with ASD may struggle to pick up on nonverbal communication, such as facial expressions, body language, and tone of voice. This can make it challenging for them to form relationships and connect with others. In addition, individuals with ASD may have trouble understanding or expressing their own emotions, which can further complicate social interactions.

Another hallmark of ASD is the presence of repetitive behaviors and restricted interests. Individuals with ASD may engage in repetitive movements, such as hand-flapping or rocking back and forth. They may also become fixated on specific topics or activities, to the exclusion of all others. While these behaviors can provide comfort and predictability for individuals with ASD, they can also interfere with daily functioning and social interaction.

Despite the challenges associated with ASD, it is important to remember that individuals with ASD have unique strengths and abilities. Many individuals with ASD have exceptional talents in areas such as music, art, mathematics, and computer science. They may also have a keen attention to detail and a strong memory for facts and figures. By recognizing and nurturing these strengths, individuals with ASD can thrive and make valuable contributions to society.

Treatment for ASD typically involves a combination of therapies and interventions tailored to the individual's specific needs. Behavioral therapy, speech therapy, occupational therapy, and social skills training are commonly used to help individuals with ASD improve their communication skills, social interactions, and daily living skills. Medication may also be prescribed to help manage symptoms such as anxiety, aggression, or hyperactivity.

In recent years, there has been a growing recognition of the importance of early intervention for individuals with ASD. Research has shown that early diagnosis and intervention can lead to better outcomes for individuals with ASD, including improved communication skills, social interactions, and academic achievement. By identifying and addressing the unique needs of individuals with ASD early on, we can help them reach their full potential and lead fulfilling lives. While the symptoms of ASD can be challenging, it is important to recognize the unique strengths and abilities of individuals with ASD. By providing targeted interventions and support, we can help individuals with ASD thrive and reach their full potential. With continued research and advocacy, we can work towards a society that is more inclusive and understanding of individuals with ASD.

- Importance of early intervention and support

Early intervention and support are essential components in ensuring the overall well-being and success of individuals, particularly children and adolescents. Research consistently shows that early intervention can significantly impact outcomes in various areas such as cognitive development, social-emotional skills, and academic achievement. By providing timely and appropriate support to individuals who may be experiencing developmental delays, learning difficulties, or emotional challenges, professionals can help mitigate the long-term effects of these issues and facilitate positive growth and development.

One of the key reasons why early intervention is so crucial is that the human brain is most malleable and responsive to intervention during the early years of life. During this critical period, the brain undergoes rapid development and is highly sensitive to environmental influences. This means that interventions implemented during the early years have the potential to shape the brain's neural circuits and support healthy development. By identifying and addressing challenges early on, professionals can help children build strong foundations for future learning, behavior, and overall well-being.

In addition to the neurobiological considerations, early intervention is also essential for addressing developmental delays and learning difficulties that may emerge during childhood. Research has shown that early identification and intervention can lead to improved outcomes in various areas, including language development, social skills, and academic performance. By providing targeted and individualized support, professionals can help children overcome challenges and reach their full potential. Early intervention can also help prevent issues from escalating and becoming more serious over time, leading to better long-term outcomes.

Furthermore, early intervention and support play a crucial role in promoting mental health and emotional well-being in children and adolescents. Young people may experience a range of emotional challenges, such as anxiety, depression, or behavioral issues, which can impact their ability to thrive in various areas of life. By providing early and appropriate support, professionals can help children and adolescents develop coping strategies, build resilience, and learn healthy ways of managing their emotions. This can help prevent the development of more serious mental health issues later in life and support overall emotional well-being.

In addition to the individual benefits, early intervention can also have broader societal impacts. Research has shown that early intervention programs can lead to long-term cost savings for society by reducing the need for more intensive and costly interventions later in life. By investing in early intervention and support services, governments and communities can promote positive outcomes for individuals, families, and society as a whole. Early intervention programs can also help reduce disparities in outcomes among different groups, ensuring that all individuals have the opportunity to thrive and succeed. By providing timely and appropriate support, professionals can help children and young people overcome challenges, build resilience, and reach their full potential. Early intervention can have a profound impact on various areas, including cognitive development, social-emotional skills, and academic achievement. By investing in early intervention programs, governments and communities can promote positive outcomes for individuals, families, and society as a whole. Ultimately, early intervention is a powerful tool for fostering healthy development and supporting the well-being of individuals across the lifespan.

- Navigating the challenges of raising a child with autism

Raising a child with autism can present unique challenges for parents, caregivers, and families. Autism Spectrum Disorder (ASD) is a developmental disorder that affects social interaction, communication, and behavior. Children with autism may have difficulty with verbal and nonverbal communication, forming relationships, and understanding the emotions of others. These challenges can impact everyday activities such as going to school, playing with peers, and participating in family gatherings.

One of the key challenges of raising a child with autism is navigating the complex healthcare system to access the resources and support needed. Parents often struggle to find the right professionals and services that can help their child with autism reach their full potential. This can involve coordinating care between various healthcare providers, therapists, educators, and community resources. It is important for parents to advocate for their child and ensure they receive the appropriate evaluations, therapies, and interventions to address their unique needs.

In addition to accessing healthcare services, parents of children with autism also face challenges in managing their child's behavior and teaching them essential life skills. Children with autism may exhibit challenging behaviors such as meltdowns, tantrums, or repetitive behaviors that can be difficult to manage. Parents may need to learn strategies for providing positive reinforcement, setting clear expectations, and teaching their child new skills in a structured and consistent manner. This can require patience, creativity, and flexibility to meet the individual needs of the child with autism.

Another challenge of raising a child with autism is navigating the education system to ensure their child receives a quality education that meets their unique needs. Children with autism may require specialized education plans, support services, and accommodations to access the curriculum and participate in school activities. Parents may need to collaborate with teachers, therapists, and school administrators to develop an Individualized Education Program (IEP) or a 504 plan that outlines the specific goals, strategies, and accommodations for their child with autism. This can involve advocating for additional supports, resources, or modifications to help their child succeed in school.

In addition to managing healthcare and education needs, parents of children with autism also face challenges in finding balance and self-care to maintain their own well-being. Raising a child with autism can be emotionally, physically, and financially demanding, which can take a toll on parents and caregivers. It is important for parents to prioritize self-care, seek support from family and friends, and access resources such as counseling or respite care to prevent burnout and maintain their own health and well-being. Taking care of oneself is essential in order to effectively support and advocate for a child with autism.

Despite the challenges of raising a child with autism, there are also opportunities for growth, learning, and connection that can positively impact families. Parents of children with autism may develop a greater sense of empathy, patience, and resilience as they navigate the ups and downs of raising a child with unique needs. They may also form close bonds with other families in the autism community who can offer support, understanding, and guidance. By seeking out resources, building a strong support network, and practicing self-care, parents can effectively navigate the challenges of raising a child with autism and help their child thrive in all aspects of life.

Chapter 2: Recognizing the Signs of Autism

- COMMON SYMPTOMS AND behaviors

Common symptoms and behaviors are often observed in individuals who are experiencing various physical or mental health conditions. These symptoms can manifest in different ways depending on the individual and the underlying cause of their condition. Understanding and recognizing these symptoms can be crucial in diagnosing and treating the individual effectively.

One of the most common symptoms that individuals may experience is fatigue. Fatigue is a feeling of constant tiredness or lack of energy that can significantly impact a person's daily life. It can be caused by a variety of factors including stress, lack of sleep, medical conditions such as anemia or thyroid disorders, or even lifestyle habits such as poor diet or excessive alcohol consumption. Recognizing fatigue in individuals is important as it can affect their ability to perform daily tasks and may indicate an underlying health issue that needs to be addressed.

Another common symptom that individuals may exhibit is changes in appetite or weight. This can manifest as either an increase or decrease in appetite, as well as unexplained weight gain or loss. Changes in appetite and weight can be indicative of a variety of health conditions such as depression, anxiety, hormonal imbalances, or gastrointestinal disorders. Monitoring an individual's eating habits and weight fluctuations can provide valuable information for healthcare professionals in diagnosing and treating the underlying cause of these symptoms.

In addition to physical symptoms, individuals may also exhibit behavioral changes that are indicative of underlying health issues. For example, changes in mood such as persistent sadness, irritability, or anger can be signs of mental health conditions such as depression or anxiety. Similarly, withdrawal from social activities, hobbies, or work may indicate that an individual is experiencing feelings of isolation or disinterest in activities that they once enjoyed. Recognizing and addressing these behavioral changes is essential in providing appropriate support and treatment for individuals experiencing mental health issues.

Furthermore, individuals may experience cognitive symptoms that affect their thinking, memory, and concentration. Cognitive symptoms can include difficulty in remembering information, making decisions, or processing thoughts. These symptoms can be indicative of neurological conditions such as dementia, Alzheimer's disease, or traumatic brain injury. Recognizing cognitive symptoms early on can help healthcare professionals intervene with appropriate treatment and support to improve an individual's cognitive functioning and quality of life.

It is important to note that symptoms and behaviors can vary widely among individuals and can be influenced by a multitude of factors such as genetics, environment, lifestyle, and personal experiences. Additionally, symptoms may also present differently in different populations such as children, older adults, or individuals with pre-existing medical conditions. Therefore, healthcare professionals must take a comprehensive and individualized approach when evaluating and addressing symptoms and behaviors in their patients. By closely monitoring changes in physical, behavioral, and cognitive symptoms, healthcare professionals can provide timely interventions and support to improve the overall health and well-being of individuals. It is important for healthcare professionals to approach each individual holistically, taking into account their unique circumstances and experiences in order to provide optimal care and support. By working collaboratively with patients and their families, healthcare professionals can help individuals navigate their symptoms and behaviors and work towards better health outcomes.

- Different forms of autism

Autism spectrum disorder (ASD) is a complex neurodevelopmental disorder that affects individuals in various ways. Within the spectrum, there are different forms of autism that present with unique characteristics and challenges. Understanding these different forms can help individuals, families, and professionals better support and accommodate individuals with autism.

One of the most well-known forms of autism is Asperger's syndrome. Individuals with Asperger's typically have average to above-average intelligence and language development, but struggle with social interactions and communication. They may have difficulty understanding social cues, maintaining eye contact, and engaging in reciprocal conversations. People with Asperger's may also have specific interests or repetitive behaviors. While they may excel in certain areas, such as math or science, they may struggle with activities that require social skills or flexibility.

Another form of autism is Pervasive Developmental Disorder-Not Otherwise Specified (PDD-NOS). This diagnosis is often given to individuals who have some, but not all, of the symptoms of autism. People with PDD-NOS may have mild social difficulties, repetitive behaviors, or restricted interests. They may also exhibit delays in language development or have unusual sensory sensitivities. While their symptoms may not meet the criteria for a diagnosis of classic autism, individuals with PDD-NOS still experience challenges in social communication and behavior.

Rett syndrome is a rare form of autism that predominantly affects girls. It is caused by a genetic mutation that affects the development of the brain. Individuals with Rett syndrome typically experience a period of normal development before regressing and losing previously acquired skills. They may exhibit repetitive hand movements, breathing difficulties, and seizures. People with Rett syndrome often require intensive support and medical care to manage their symptoms and maintain their quality of life.

Childhood Disintegrative Disorder (CDD) is another rare form of autism that involves significant regression in multiple areas of development, such as language, social skills, and daily living skills. Children with CDD may lose previously acquired abilities, such as toilet training or language skills, and may exhibit a decline in overall functioning. This regression typically occurs between the ages of 2 and 10 years old, leading to a diagnosis of CDD. While the cause of CDD is not fully understood, it is believed to involve a combination of genetic and environmental factors.

To sum up, there is the classic form of autism, also known as autistic disorder or autism spectrum disorder. Individuals with classic autism typically exhibit difficulties in social communication, repetitive behaviors, and restricted interests. They may struggle with eye contact, nonverbal communication, and understanding social norms. People with classic autism may also have sensory sensitivities, such as being hypo- or hypersensitive to certain stimuli. While individuals with classic autism have a diverse range of strengths and challenges, they often require support in areas of communication, social skills, and behavior management. Asperger's syndrome, PDD-NOS, Rett syndrome, Childhood Disintegrative Disorder, and classic autism all present with varying degrees of social communication difficulties, repetitive behaviors, and sensory sensitivities. Understanding these different forms of autism can help individuals, families, and professionals provide appropriate support and interventions to improve the quality of life for individuals with autism. By recognizing the diversity within the autism spectrum, we can ensure that individuals with autism receive the individualized support and accommodations they need to thrive.

- Early diagnosis and intervention

Early diagnosis and intervention are crucial components of effective healthcare management, especially when it comes to detecting and treating various medical conditions. Early diagnosis refers to the identification of a disease or condition at its initial stages, often before symptoms become apparent. This can significantly improve patient outcomes and quality of life by enabling timely and appropriate treatment. Intervention, on the other hand, involves taking action to address the identified issues through medical, psychological, or other forms of support.

One of the key benefits of early diagnosis and intervention is the ability to prevent the progression of a disease or condition. By catching a medical issue early on, healthcare providers can implement strategies to slow down or even reverse its advancement. For example, early detection of cancer allows for prompt treatment, which can increase the chances of successful outcomes. Similarly, early intervention in developmental delays in children can help minimize the long-term effects of these challenges on their growth and well-being.

Another advantage of early diagnosis and intervention is the potential to reduce healthcare costs in the long run. By addressing health concerns early, patients may require less intensive and costly treatments down the line. This can result in significant savings for both individuals and healthcare systems. Additionally, early intervention can help prevent complications that may arise from untreated conditions, further reducing medical expenses and improving overall outcomes.

Early diagnosis and intervention also play a critical role in improving the overall quality of life for individuals affected by various health conditions. By addressing issues early, patients can better manage their symptoms and maintain a higher level of functioning. This can have a positive impact on their mental, emotional, and social well-being, as well as their ability to engage in daily activities. For example, early intervention for individuals with autism spectrum disorder can help them develop essential skills and improve their overall quality of life.

In addition to individual benefits, early diagnosis and intervention can also have broader societal impacts. By identifying and addressing health issues early, healthcare providers can help prevent the spread of diseases and reduce the overall burden on healthcare systems. This can contribute to a healthier population and more efficient use of resources. Furthermore, early intervention can improve educational outcomes for children with developmental delays, allowing them to reach their full potential and contribute to society in meaningful ways.

Despite the clear advantages of early diagnosis and intervention, there are still challenges that need to be addressed to optimize their effectiveness. One of the key barriers is the lack of awareness and access to screening and diagnostic tools, especially in underserved communities. Improving education and outreach efforts, as well as increasing resources for early detection programs, can help address this issue. Additionally, healthcare providers must be trained to recognize the signs and symptoms of various conditions and to implement timely interventions. By detecting and addressing health issues early, providers can improve patient outcomes, reduce healthcare costs, and enhance the overall quality of life for individuals affected by various medical conditions. It is crucial for healthcare systems to prioritize early detection and intervention efforts to maximize their impact and promote the well-being of their communities.

Chapter 3: Getting a Diagnosis

- STEPS TO TAKE FOR a formal diagnosis

Obtaining a formal diagnosis for any medical condition is a crucial step in receiving appropriate treatment and support. When it comes to mental health disorders, seeking a formal diagnosis is equally important in order to access the right interventions and therapy. If you suspect that you or a loved one may be experiencing symptoms of a mental health condition, taking the necessary steps to obtain a formal diagnosis is essential.

The first step in obtaining a formal diagnosis for a mental health disorder is to schedule an appointment with a healthcare provider. This could be a general practitioner, psychiatrist, psychologist, or counselor. During the initial appointment, it is important to be open and honest about your symptoms and concerns. Providing a detailed history of your symptoms, including when they started, how they have progressed, and any triggers or patterns you have noticed, can help the healthcare provider make an accurate diagnosis.

After discussing your symptoms and concerns with a healthcare provider, they may recommend further assessment or testing to gather more information. This could include psychological assessments, blood tests, or imaging studies. These additional tests can help rule out other medical conditions that may be causing or contributing to your symptoms. It is important to follow through with any recommended testing in order to obtain a comprehensive evaluation.

Once all necessary assessments and testing have been completed, the healthcare provider will review the results and make a formal diagnosis. This diagnosis will be based on the criteria outlined in the Diagnostic and Statistical Manual of Mental Disorders (DSM-5), which is the standard classification system used by healthcare providers to diagnose mental health disorders. The

DSM-5 outlines specific criteria for each mental health disorder, including the symptoms that must be present and the duration and severity of those symptoms.

After receiving a formal diagnosis, the healthcare provider will work with you to develop a treatment plan. This plan may include medication, therapy, lifestyle changes, or a combination of interventions. It is important to follow the treatment plan as prescribed in order to manage your symptoms and improve your overall well-being. In some cases, the healthcare provider may also refer you to a specialist for further evaluation or treatment.

In addition to following the treatment plan provided by your healthcare provider, it is important to engage in self-care activities that support your mental health. This could include regular exercise, healthy eating, stress management techniques, and engaging in activities that bring you joy and relaxation. Building a strong support system of friends, family, and mental health professionals can also help you navigate the challenges of living with a mental health disorder. By scheduling an appointment with a healthcare provider, completing any necessary assessments and testing, receiving a formal diagnosis based on the DSM-5 criteria, and following a personalized treatment plan, you can take proactive steps to manage your symptoms and improve your quality of life. In addition to following the treatment plan, engaging in self-care activities and building a strong support system can help you navigate the challenges of living with a mental health disorder. By prioritizing your mental health and seeking the necessary support, you can take control of your well-being and thrive despite the challenges you may face.

- Working with healthcare professionals

Working with healthcare professionals requires a combination of effective communication, collaboration, and professionalism. Healthcare professionals come from various backgrounds and specialties, each bringing their unique expertise and skills to the table. It is essential to approach these collaborations with an open mind and a willingness to learn from others.

One of the key aspects of working with healthcare professionals is establishing clear lines of communication. This includes not only conveying information effectively but also actively listening to the perspectives and insights of others. Clear communication ensures that everyone is on the same page and can work together towards common goals. Whether it's discussing a patient's treatment plan or coordinating care across different specialties, effective communication is crucial in the healthcare setting.

Collaboration is another crucial component of working with healthcare professionals. In today's healthcare landscape, many patients require interdisciplinary care involving multiple specialties and healthcare professionals. Collaborating with others allows for a holistic approach to patient care, where different perspectives and expertise can come together to provide the best possible outcomes for patients. This collaboration can take many forms, from regular team meetings to joint decision-making on patient care plans.

Professionalism is the foundation of any successful working relationship with healthcare professionals. This means treating others with respect, maintaining confidentiality, and adhering to ethical standards and guidelines. In the fast-paced and high-stress environment of healthcare, professionalism is essential to ensuring that all members of the healthcare team can work together effectively and efficiently. It also sets a standard for the quality of care provided to patients, as professionalism fosters a culture of excellence and accountability.

As a healthcare professional, it is important to approach collaborations with an open mind and a willingness to learn from others. Every healthcare professional brings their unique expertise and insights to the table, and by working together, we can all benefit from shared knowledge and experiences. This collaborative approach not only leads to better patient outcomes but also helps to foster a supportive and inclusive work environment where everyone's contributions are valued. By establishing clear lines of communication, collaborating with others, and maintaining a high standard of professionalism, we can work together to provide the best possible care for our patients. Approaching collaborations with an open mind and a willingness to learn from others can help us to achieve better outcomes and create a positive work environment where everyone's contributions are valued. Together, we can make a difference in the lives of our patients and continue to improve the quality of healthcare for all.

- Managing emotions and expectations

Managing emotions and expectations is a critical skill that is essential for success in both personal and professional settings. Emotions are a natural part of being human, and they play a significant role in shaping our thoughts, behaviors, and interactions with others. However, when emotions are not effectively managed, they can lead to irrational decision-making, conflict, and stress. By learning to regulate our emotions and set realistic expectations, we can enhance our overall well-being and improve our relationships with others.

One of the key aspects of managing emotions is recognizing and acknowledging them in the first place. Many people try to suppress or ignore their emotions, believing that this will make them go away. However, this only serves to bottle up emotions, leading to more intense and uncontrollable outbursts later on. Instead, it is important to take the time to identify and understand what we are feeling, whether it be anger, sadness, fear, or joy. By acknowledging our emotions, we can begin to address them in a constructive and healthy manner.

Once we have identified our emotions, the next step is to regulate them effectively. This involves taking a step back and assessing the situation objectively, rather than reacting impulsively based on our initial emotions. It can be helpful to practice mindfulness techniques, such as deep breathing or progressive muscle relaxation, to calm the mind and body before responding. Additionally, it is important to consider the potential consequences of our actions and choose a response that is appropriate and beneficial in the long run.

In addition to managing our own emotions, it is also important to be mindful of the emotions of others. Empathy plays a crucial role in effective communication and conflict resolution, as it allows us to understand and connect with the feelings and perspectives of those around us. By listening actively, showing understanding, and validating the emotions of others, we can build trust and strengthen our relationships. This can be particularly important in professional settings, where effective collaboration and teamwork are essential for success.

Setting realistic expectations is another key component of managing emotions and fostering positive relationships. It is important to be honest with ourselves and others about what we can realistically achieve and how we can realistically feel. Unrealistic expectations can lead to disappointment, frustration, and resentment, both for ourselves and for those around us. By setting clear and achievable goals, we can reduce stress and improve our overall well-being.

Communication is a crucial aspect of managing expectations, as it allows us to express our needs and boundaries effectively. It is important to be assertive yet respectful in our communication, making sure to listen to the needs and perspectives of others as well. By setting clear boundaries and managing expectations proactively, we can prevent misunderstandings and conflicts from arising. Effective communication can also help us to build trust and strengthen our relationships with others, both in personal and professional settings. By acknowledging and regulating our emotions, showing empathy towards others, setting realistic expectations, and communicating effectively, we can improve our well-being, strengthen our relationships, and enhance our overall quality of life. By recognizing the importance of emotional intelligence and taking proactive steps to develop this skill, we can navigate the complexities of human emotions with grace and maturity.

Chapter 4: Understanding Treatment Options

- OVERVIEW OF THERAPIES and interventions

These interventions can take many forms, ranging from traditional talk therapy to more innovative and holistic approaches. In this overview, we will explore the different types of therapies and interventions available, their goals, and how they can be effectively utilized to help individuals overcome challenges and thrive in their daily lives.

One of the most common forms of therapy is cognitive-behavioral therapy (CBT), which focuses on helping individuals identify and change negative thought patterns and behaviors that contribute to their mental health issues. CBT is a structured and goal-oriented approach that is often used to treat conditions such as anxiety disorders, depression, and post-traumatic stress disorder.

Another commonly used therapy is psychodynamic therapy, which is rooted in the idea that past experiences and unconscious motivations influence our current thoughts, feelings, and behaviors. Psychodynamic therapy involves exploring and gaining insight into these underlying issues through open-ended conversations with a therapist. By uncovering and processing these unresolved conflicts, individuals can gain a greater understanding of themselves and make positive changes in their lives.

In addition to traditional forms of therapy, there are a variety of alternative and complementary interventions that can be helpful in promoting mental health and well-being. By learning to cultivate a present-moment awareness, individuals can develop greater self-awareness and acceptance, leading to a greater sense of peace and well-being.

Art therapy is another alternative intervention that can be beneficial for individuals struggling with emotional and psychological issues. Through the use of artistic expression, individuals can explore their thoughts and feelings in a safe and creative way. Art therapy can be particularly helpful for those who have difficulty expressing themselves verbally or who may benefit from a more hands-on approach to therapy.

In addition to individual therapy, there are also group therapy and support groups that can be valuable in promoting mental health and well-being. Group therapy allows individuals to connect with others who may be experiencing similar challenges, providing a sense of community and support. Support groups, on the other hand, offer a more informal setting for individuals to share their experiences, gain insights, and receive encouragement from others who can relate to their struggles. Whether through traditional talk therapy, alternative approaches such as mindfulness and art therapy, or group settings, individuals can find the support and tools they need to overcome challenges and thrive in their daily lives. By understanding the different types of therapies and interventions available, individuals can make informed decisions about the best approach for their unique needs and goals.

- Finding the right approach for your child

For parents, finding the right approach for their child can often feel like navigating a maze with no clear path. There are so many different methods, philosophies, and theories out there about how to best raise and educate children, and it can be overwhelming to try and figure out what will work best for your own child. However, by taking a step back and considering your child's unique needs, personality, and learning style, you can start to tailor your approach in a way that is most effective for them.

One key factor to consider when trying to find the right approach for your child is their individual temperament. Some children are naturally more introverted and may thrive in a quiet, structured environment, while others are more extroverted and need frequent social interaction and stimulation. Understanding your child's temperament can help you tailor your parenting and educational strategies to better meet their needs and help them succeed.

Another important factor to consider is your child's learning style. Some children are visual learners, while others learn best through auditory or kinesthetic means. By identifying your child's learning style, you can adapt your approach to better suit their needs and help them retain information more effectively. For example, if your child is a visual learner, incorporating more visual aids and activities into their learning can help them grasp concepts more readily.

It's also important to consider your child's interests and passions when determining the right approach for them. If your child is particularly interested in science, for example, incorporating more science-related activities and materials into their education can help keep them engaged and motivated. By aligning your approach with your child's interests, you can help foster a love of learning and encourage them to explore new areas of interest.

Additionally, it's important to be flexible and open to trying different approaches as your child grows and develops. What may work well for your child at one stage of their development may not be as effective at another stage. By staying attuned to your child's changing needs and adjusting your approach accordingly, you can better support their growth and development. By tailoring your approach to best meet your child's needs and preferences, you can help them thrive and succeed. Remember to stay flexible and open to trying new strategies as your child grows and develops, and don't be afraid to seek support from educators, therapists, or other professionals if needed. With the right approach, you can help your child reach their full potential and set them up for future success.

- Support services and resources available

Support services and resources are vital components of any community or organization, as they provide assistance and guidance to individuals who may be experiencing challenges or facing obstacles in their lives. These services are designed to help people overcome difficulties, improve their quality of life, and achieve their goals. In this article, we will explore the various support services and resources that are available to individuals in need, and discuss the benefits of accessing these services.

One of the most common support services available to individuals is counseling or therapy. Counseling is a form of mental health support that involves talking to a trained professional about your thoughts, feelings, and emotions. This type of support can be beneficial for individuals who are experiencing stress, anxiety, depression, or other mental health issues. Counseling can help individuals develop coping strategies, improve their self-esteem, and work through difficult emotions. Therapy sessions are typically conducted in a confidential and safe environment, allowing individuals to freely express themselves without fear of judgment.

Another important support service available to individuals is case management. Case managers work with individuals to assess their needs, develop a plan for addressing those needs, and connect them with resources and services that can help them achieve their goals. Case managers may work with individuals who are experiencing homelessness, substance abuse issues, or mental health challenges. They can help individuals access housing, medical care, job training, and other essential services. Case managers also provide ongoing support to help individuals stay on track and make progress towards their goals.

In addition to counseling and case management, there are a variety of other support services and resources available to individuals in need. These may include support groups, crisis hotlines, legal assistance, financial counseling, and vocational training programs. Support groups provide individuals with a sense of community and connection, allowing them to share their experiences and learn from others who are facing similar challenges. Crisis hotlines are available 24/7 to provide immediate support to individuals who are in crisis or experiencing a mental health emergency. Legal assistance can help individuals navigate the legal system and access the resources they need to address legal issues. Financial counseling can help individuals create budgets, manage debt, and improve their financial literacy. Vocational training programs can help individuals develop the skills they need to secure employment and achieve financial stability.

Accessing support services and resources can have a positive impact on individuals' lives. Research has shown that individuals who receive support services are more likely to achieve their goals, improve their mental health, and increase their overall well-being. By accessing counseling, case management, support groups, crisis hotlines, legal assistance, financial counseling, and vocational training programs, individuals can build the skills and resources they need to overcome challenges and thrive. Support services can provide individuals with the tools they need to create positive change in their lives and build a brighter future. These services are designed to help individuals overcome challenges, improve their quality of life, and achieve their goals. By accessing counseling, case management, support groups, crisis hotlines, legal assistance, financial counseling, and vocational training programs, individuals can build the skills and resources they need to create positive change in their lives. It is important for individuals to know that support is available and to reach out for help when needed. By seeking support, individuals can take proactive steps towards improving their mental health, well-being, and overall quality of life.

Chapter 5: Creating a Supportive Environment

- BUILDING A ROUTINE and structure

Building a routine and structure is crucial for achieving success and maintaining a balance in one's life. By following a set schedule and creating a framework for daily activities, individuals can increase productivity, reduce stress, and improve overall well-being. Establishing a routine involves setting specific goals, prioritizing tasks, and creating a consistent schedule to follow each day.

One of the key benefits of building a routine and structure is the ability to manage time effectively. By breaking down tasks into smaller, manageable chunks and allocating time for each one, individuals can ensure that they are making progress towards their goals. This can help prevent procrastination and ensure that important tasks are completed in a timely manner. Additionally, having a structured routine can help individuals avoid feeling overwhelmed by their workload, as they can focus on one task at a time and make steady progress towards their objectives.

In addition to managing time effectively, building a routine and structure can also help individuals improve their focus and concentration. By establishing a set schedule for work, study, and other activities, individuals can eliminate distractions and create a conducive environment for productivity. This can lead to better performance in tasks, improved learning outcomes, and increased efficiency in completing projects. Having a routine can also help individuals establish healthy habits, such as regular exercise, adequate sleep, and balanced meals, which can contribute to overall well-being and productivity.

Another important aspect of building a routine and structure is the ability to create a sense of stability and predictability in one's life. Having a set schedule can provide a sense of security and comfort, as individuals know what to expect each day and can plan their activities accordingly. This can help reduce stress and anxiety, as individuals are less likely to be caught off guard by unexpected events or changes in their routine. Additionally, having a structured routine can help individuals build resilience and adaptability, as they are better prepared to handle challenges and setbacks that may arise.

Building a routine and structure can also help individuals achieve a better work-life balance. By setting boundaries between work and personal time, individuals can ensure that they have time for relaxation, social activities, and self-care. This can prevent burnout and reduce the risk of physical and mental health issues associated with overwork. Having a structured routine can also help individuals prioritize their well-being and relationships, leading to a more fulfilling and balanced life overall. By establishing a set schedule, prioritizing tasks, and creating a framework for daily activities, individuals can improve their time management, focus, and productivity. Additionally, having a routine can help individuals create stability, predictability, and balance in their lives, leading to better overall well-being and fulfillment. By incorporating healthy habits, setting boundaries, and prioritizing self-care, individuals can build a routine that supports their goals, enhances their productivity, and contributes to their overall happiness and success.

- Enhancing communication and social skills

Enhancing communication and social skills is a crucial aspect of personal and professional development. Effective communication skills are essential for building strong relationships, both in the workplace and in personal interactions. Social skills, on the other hand, refer to the ability to interact with others in a positive and productive manner. Both of these skills are interconnected and play a significant role in one's overall success and well-being.

Effective communication involves more than just speaking clearly and concisely. It also involves listening actively and empathetically to others. Good communication requires the ability to convey your thoughts and ideas clearly and in a manner that is easily understood by others. This involves using appropriate language, tone, and body language to convey your message effectively. Additionally, effective communication also involves being able to understand and interpret the thoughts, feelings, and ideas of others.

Social skills, on the other hand, refer to the ability to interact with others in a positive and productive manner. This involves being able to build and maintain relationships, resolve conflicts, and work effectively in a team setting. Social skills also include the ability to read social cues, understand others' emotions, and respond appropriately in social situations. Developing strong social skills can help you build strong relationships, gain the trust and respect of others, and navigate social interactions with confidence.

There are several strategies that can help individuals enhance their communication and social skills. One of the most important strategies is to practice active listening. Active listening involves fully engaging with the speaker, paying attention to their words, tone, and body language, and responding in a way that shows that you understand and care about what they are saying. Active listening can help improve communication by ensuring that both parties feel heard and understood.

Another important strategy for enhancing communication and social skills is to practice effective nonverbal communication. Nonverbal communication includes gestures, facial expressions, and body language, and can have a significant impact on how your message is perceived. By being aware of your nonverbal cues and making an effort to use them effectively, you can enhance your communication and social interactions.

Additionally, developing empathy is essential for enhancing communication and social skills. Empathy involves putting yourself in another person's shoes and understanding their thoughts, feelings, and perspectives. By developing empathy, you can improve your ability to connect with others, build relationships, and resolve conflicts in a positive and productive manner.

To terminate, seeking feedback and actively working to improve your communication and social skills is essential for growth and development. By seeking feedback from others, you can gain insight into how you are perceived by others and identify areas for improvement. Actively working to improve your communication and social skills can help you build stronger relationships, advance in your career, and achieve your personal and professional goals. Effective communication and social skills can help you build strong relationships, communicate effectively, and navigate social interactions with confidence. By practicing active listening, using effective nonverbal communication, developing empathy, and seeking feedback, you can enhance your communication and social skills and achieve success in all areas of your life.

- Addressing sensory sensitivities

Addressing sensory sensitivities is an important aspect of accommodating diverse needs in various environments, including schools, workplaces, and public spaces. Sensory sensitivities refer to heightened responses to sensory stimuli, such as loud noises, bright lights, strong smells, or certain textures. Individuals with sensory sensitivities may experience discomfort, anxiety, or even physical pain when exposed to these triggers. It is essential to create a supportive and inclusive environment for individuals with sensory sensitivities by implementing strategies that help minimize sensory overload and promote a sense of safety and well-being.

One effective way to address sensory sensitivities is through environmental modifications. For example, in a classroom setting, dimming lights, reducing background noise, and providing sensory-friendly materials can help create a more comfortable learning environment for students with sensory sensitivities. Employers can also make adjustments in the workplace, such as providing noise-canceling headphones, allowing for flexible workspaces, or establishing quiet zones for employees who may be sensitive to certain stimuli. By making simple changes to the physical environment, organizations can create a more inclusive space that supports individuals with sensory sensitivities.

In addition to environmental modifications, it is important to provide individuals with sensory sensitivities with the necessary tools and resources to self-regulate and cope with sensory challenges. This can include offering sensory-friendly tools, such as fidget toys, weighted blankets, or noise-canceling headphones, to help individuals manage their sensory experiences. Additionally, teaching individuals coping strategies, such as deep breathing exercises, mindfulness techniques, or sensory breaks, can empower them to better navigate overwhelming sensory stimuli. By equipping individuals with the skills and resources needed to self-regulate, we can support their overall well-being and success in various settings.

Another key aspect of addressing sensory sensitivities is promoting awareness and understanding among peers, colleagues, and the general public. It is important to educate others about sensory sensitivities and the diverse ways in which individuals may experience them. By fostering a culture of empathy and acceptance, we can create a more inclusive and supportive community for individuals with sensory sensitivities. This may involve providing training sessions, workshops, or informational materials to raise awareness and encourage understanding of the unique challenges faced by individuals with sensory sensitivities. By promoting a more inclusive and understanding environment, we can help reduce stigma and create a more inclusive society for all individuals.

Furthermore, it is important to collaborate with individuals with sensory sensitivities and their families to develop individualized support plans that address their specific needs and preferences. By involving individuals in the decision-making process, we can ensure that their voices are heard and that their unique needs are taken into account. This person-centered approach allows for a more tailored and effective support system that reflects the individual's strengths, preferences, and goals. By working together with individuals and their families, we can create a supportive and empowering environment that promotes their overall well-being and success. By implementing environmental modifications, providing tools and resources for self-regulation, promoting awareness and understanding, and collaborating with individuals and their families, we can create a more inclusive society that respects and accommodates the unique needs of all individuals. By taking a proactive and person-centered approach to addressing sensory sensitivities, we can help individuals with sensory sensitivities thrive and reach their full potential in school, work, and community settings.

Chapter 6: Building Relationships and Social Skills

- HELPING YOUR CHILD connect with others

Helping your child connect with others is an essential aspect of their social and emotional development. By fostering healthy relationships with peers, siblings, and adults, children can learn important skills such as communication, empathy, and cooperation. As a parent, it is important to provide opportunities for your child to interact with others in a positive and supportive environment. This can help them build confidence and self-esteem, as well as develop a sense of belonging and connectedness to the world around them.

One of the key ways to help your child connect with others is to encourage and model appropriate social behaviors. Children learn by observing the actions of those around them, so it is important for parents to demonstrate kindness, respect, and empathy in their own interactions with others. By treating others with compassion and understanding, parents can set a positive example for their children to follow. Additionally, parents can help their children develop important social skills such as active listening, taking turns, and expressing emotions in a healthy way.

Another important aspect of helping your child connect with others is providing opportunities for them to socialize and build relationships. This can include organizing playdates with other children, enrolling them in extracurricular activities such as sports or music lessons, or encouraging them to participate in group activities at school or in the community. By exposing your child to a variety of social settings, you can help them develop the confidence and social skills needed to navigate different social situations and build meaningful connections with others.

It is also important for parents to create a supportive and nurturing environment for their child to express themselves and share their thoughts and feelings with others. By creating a safe space for open communication, parents can help their children develop the emotional intelligence needed to form healthy relationships with their peers. Parents can also help their children understand and navigate social conflicts by teaching them problem-solving skills and encouraging them to communicate their needs and boundaries assertively.

In addition to providing opportunities for socialization and fostering open communication, parents can also help their children develop empathy and understanding towards others. By teaching children to consider the perspectives and feelings of those around them, parents can help their children develop a sense of empathy and compassion towards others. Children who are able to empathize with others are more likely to form strong and meaningful relationships with their peers, as they are able to understand and respect the emotions and experiences of those around them. By fostering healthy relationships and providing opportunities for socialization, parents can help their children develop the social skills, empathy, and confidence needed to form meaningful connections with their peers. By creating a supportive and nurturing environment for open communication and empathy, parents can help their children navigate social situations and build strong and lasting relationships with others. By investing time and effort into helping your child connect with others, you can help them develop the social skills and emotional intelligence needed to thrive in their relationships and interactions with others.

- Teaching social cues and interactions

Teaching social cues and interactions is a crucial aspect of education that encompasses not only verbal communication but also nonverbal gestures and body language. As humans are social beings, the ability to navigate social interactions effectively is essential for personal and professional success. In today's fast-paced and interconnected world, the importance of understanding and interpreting social cues cannot be overstated. Whether in a classroom setting, a job interview, or a casual gathering with friends, being able to pick up on social cues and respond appropriately can greatly enhance one's relationships and overall well-being.

One of the key components of teaching social cues and interactions is fostering emotional intelligence. Emotional intelligence refers to the ability to recognize, understand, and manage one's own emotions as well as the emotions of others. By developing emotional intelligence, individuals can better navigate social situations and build stronger relationships. Educators can help students develop emotional intelligence by teaching them to recognize their own emotions and the emotions of others, as well as how to respond empathetically and effectively in various social settings.

In addition to emotional intelligence, teaching social cues and interactions also involves helping students understand cultural differences and nuances in communication. In today's diverse society, it is essential for individuals to be aware of and sensitive to the cultural backgrounds and communication styles of others. Educators can facilitate this by exposing students to different cultural perspectives and providing opportunities for them to engage in cross-cultural interactions. By teaching students to approach social interactions with an open mind and a willingness to learn from others, educators can help foster a more inclusive and understanding society.

Furthermore, teaching social cues and interactions can also involve role-playing exercises and real-life scenarios to help students practice and refine their social skills. By engaging students in hands-on activities that mimic real-world social situations, educators can provide them with valuable opportunities to apply and reinforce their learning. Role-playing exercises can also help students develop their problem-solving abilities and build confidence in their social interactions. By incorporating these practical techniques into their teaching, educators can help students gain the skills and confidence they need to navigate social cues and interactions successfully in a variety of settings.

It is also important for educators to provide ongoing support and feedback to students as they work to improve their social cues and interactions. By offering constructive feedback and guidance, educators can help students identify areas for improvement and develop strategies for enhancing their social skills. Providing a safe and supportive environment where students feel comfortable experimenting with new social cues and interactions is crucial for fostering growth and development. Educators can also encourage students to seek out opportunities for mentorship and peer support, which can further enhance their learning and growth in this area. By fostering emotional intelligence, promoting cross-cultural understanding, incorporating practical exercises, and offering ongoing support and feedback, educators can help students develop the skills and confidence they need to navigate social interactions successfully. By equipping students with the tools and knowledge to interpret social cues and communicate effectively, educators can empower them to forge stronger relationships, succeed in their careers, and contribute positively to society.

- Navigating friendships and relationships

Friendships and relationships are an essential component of human life, providing support, companionship, and emotional connection. Navigating these social connections can be both rewarding and challenging, as they require time, effort, and effective communication. In this discussion, we will explore some key strategies for navigating friendships and relationships successfully, including setting boundaries, practicing empathy, and maintaining open and honest communication.

One of the most important aspects of navigating friendships and relationships is setting clear boundaries. Boundaries are essential for maintaining healthy and respectful relationships, as they help define what is and is not acceptable behavior. Setting boundaries can help prevent misunderstandings, conflicts, and hurt feelings by establishing guidelines for how you expect to be treated and how you will treat others. It is important to communicate your boundaries openly and assertively, while also being respectful of the boundaries of others. By setting and respecting boundaries, you can create a foundation of trust and mutual respect in your friendships and relationships.

In addition to setting boundaries, practicing empathy is another key strategy for navigating friendships and relationships successfully. Empathy is the ability to understand and share the feelings of another person, and it plays a crucial role in building strong and meaningful connections with others. By putting yourself in the shoes of your friends and loved ones, you can develop a deeper understanding of their thoughts, feelings, and perspectives. This can help you respond more effectively to their needs and concerns, strengthen your emotional bond, and foster greater trust and support in your relationships.

Practicing empathy can also help resolve conflicts and improve communication by promoting understanding and compassion.

Maintaining open and honest communication is also essential for navigating friendships and relationships effectively. Communication is the foundation of any successful relationship, allowing you to express your thoughts, feelings, and needs, as well as listen to and understand those of others. By communicating openly and honestly with your friends and loved ones, you can build trust, resolve conflicts, and strengthen your emotional bond. It is important to be transparent about your feelings and intentions, as well as to actively listen to the perspectives and concerns of others. Effective communication requires patience, active listening, and a willingness to be vulnerable, but it can lead to greater intimacy, understanding, and connection in your friendships and relationships. By setting boundaries, practicing empathy, and maintaining open and honest communication, you can cultivate trust, respect, and understanding in your friendships and relationships. Remember to prioritize self-care and prioritize your emotional well-being, as healthy relationships start with a healthy relationship with yourself. By investing time, effort, and compassion into your social connections, you can create meaningful and rewarding friendships and relationships that enrich your life and support your personal growth.

Chapter 7: School and Education Support

- ADVOCATING FOR YOUR child's educational needs

Advocating for your child's educational needs is an essential part of ensuring they receive the support and resources necessary to thrive in their academic journey. As a parent, you play a critical role in advocating for your child's education and partnering with teachers, administrators, and other stakeholders to create a supportive and conducive learning environment. Advocacy involves speaking up for your child's needs, understanding their rights, and collaborating with educators to address any challenges or barriers they may face in their educational experience.

One of the key aspects of advocating for your child's educational needs is being informed and knowledgeable about their individual strengths, weaknesses, and learning style. By understanding your child's unique needs and abilities, you can effectively communicate with teachers and school personnel about how best to support them in the classroom. This may involve discussing any learning disabilities, special accommodations, or support services that your child may require to succeed academically. By being well-informed about your child's educational needs, you can more effectively advocate on their behalf and ensure they receive the appropriate resources and support.

In addition to being informed about your child's needs, it is important to establish open lines of communication with teachers and school administrators to discuss any concerns or issues that may arise. Building a strong relationship with your child's educators can help facilitate productive discussions about their progress, challenges, and any additional support they may require. By working collaboratively with teachers and school personnel, you can develop a plan to address your child's educational needs and implement strategies to help them succeed in the classroom.

Advocating for your child's education also involves understanding their rights and entitlements under the law. It is important to familiarize yourself with federal and state laws, such as the Individuals with Disabilities Education Act (IDEA) and Section 504 of the Rehabilitation Act, which provide protections and support for students with disabilities. These laws outline the rights of students to receive a free and appropriate public education, as well as access to special education services and accommodations. By understanding your child's legal rights, you can advocate more effectively for the support and resources they are entitled to receive.

Another important aspect of advocating for your child's educational needs is being proactive and persistent in seeking out assistance and resources. If you believe your child is not receiving the support they need in the classroom, it is important to speak up and advocate for the necessary accommodations or services. This may involve requesting a meeting with teachers or school administrators to discuss your concerns, seeking out additional support services or evaluations, or exploring other options to address your child's educational needs. By being proactive in advocating for your child, you can ensure they receive the assistance and resources necessary to excel academically. By being informed, proactive, and persistent in advocating for your child, you can help ensure they receive the support and resources necessary to thrive in the classroom. By working collaboratively with teachers, administrators, and other stakeholders, you can create a supportive and inclusive learning environment that meets the individual needs of your child. Advocating for your child's education requires dedication, perseverance, and a commitment to their academic success. By being an active and engaged advocate for your child, you can help empower them to achieve their full potential and succeed in their educational journey.

- Finding the right school and classroom environment

Finding the right school and classroom environment is a critical decision that can greatly impact a student's academic success and overall experience. When considering which school to attend, it is important to take into account a variety of factors, including the school's mission and values, academic programs and offerings, location, size, student demographics, extracurricular activities, and facilities. Additionally, it is important to consider the classroom environment, as this can play a significant role in a student's motivation, engagement, and learning outcomes.

One key consideration when researching schools is the school's mission and values. It is important to choose a school whose mission aligns with your own values and beliefs. For example, if you value diversity and inclusivity, you may want to choose a school that emphasizes these principles in their mission statement and curriculum. Additionally, it is important to consider the school's academic programs and offerings. Look for schools that offer a wide range of programs and extracurricular activities that align with your interests and goals.

Location is another important factor to consider when choosing a school. Consider how far you are willing to commute to school each day, as well as the accessibility of public transportation and parking options. Additionally, consider the size of the school and student demographics. Some students may thrive in a smaller, more intimate school environment, while others may prefer a larger, more diverse student body.

When evaluating potential schools, it is also important to consider the classroom environment. A positive classroom environment can greatly impact a student's learning experience, motivation, and overall well-being. Look for schools that prioritize creating a supportive and inclusive classroom environment where students feel safe, respected, and valued.

One key aspect of a positive classroom environment is the relationship between teachers and students. Look for schools that have a strong emphasis on building positive relationships between teachers and students, as this can greatly impact a student's academic success and overall well-being. Additionally, consider the school's discipline policies and practices. A school that has clear and consistent discipline policies in place can help create a positive and safe classroom environment for all students.

Another important aspect of the classroom environment to consider is the physical space. Look for schools that have well-maintained and clean classrooms, as well as facilities that support student learning and engagement. Additionally, consider the availability of resources and technology in the classroom, as these can greatly impact a student's learning experience. By researching schools that align with your values and goals, prioritizing a positive and inclusive classroom environment, and considering key factors such as location, size, and resources, you can find a school that meets your needs and sets you up for academic success. Remember that finding the right school is a personal decision that should be based on what is best for you as a student. By taking the time to research and visit potential schools, you can make an informed decision that will set you up for success in your academic journey.

- Working with teachers and school staff

Working with teachers and school staff is a crucial aspect of ensuring the success and growth of students. Teachers and school staff play a vital role in shaping the educational experience of students and influencing their academic and personal development. As such, it is essential for administrators, support staff, and other stakeholders to collaborate effectively with teachers and school staff to create a positive and productive learning environment.

One of the key factors in working with teachers and school staff is communication. Clear and open communication is essential for building strong relationships and promoting collaboration among all members of the school community. Administrators should establish regular channels of communication with teachers and school staff, such as staff meetings, email updates, and one-on-one conversations, to keep everyone informed and engaged in the decision-making process. Effective communication helps to foster trust and mutual respect among all stakeholders, which is essential for creating a supportive and cohesive school culture.

Collaboration is another important aspect of working with teachers and school staff. Collaborating with teachers and school staff allows for the sharing of knowledge, ideas, and resources to improve teaching practices and enhance student learning outcomes. Administrators should actively involve teachers and school staff in decision-making processes, curriculum development, and school improvement initiatives to leverage their expertise and experience in shaping the direction of the school. By working together as a team, administrators, teachers, and school staff can create a unified front focused on promoting the success and well-being of all students.

Supporting teachers and school staff is also crucial for creating a positive and effective learning environment. Teachers and school staff face numerous challenges in their roles, from managing classroom behavior to meeting the diverse needs of students. Administrators should provide ongoing support and professional development opportunities for teachers and school staff to help them build their skills, knowledge, and confidence in their roles. By investing in the professional growth of teachers and school staff, administrators can empower them to deliver high-quality instruction and support for students, ultimately leading to improved academic achievement and well-being.

Recognizing and celebrating the contributions of teachers and school staff is essential for boosting morale and fostering a positive school culture. Administrators should acknowledge and appreciate the hard work and dedication of teachers and school staff through formal recognition programs, personalized notes of thanks, and staff appreciation events. By showing appreciation for the efforts and achievements of teachers and school staff, administrators can create a sense of camaraderie and unity within the school community, which can have a positive impact on employee motivation and job satisfaction. By prioritizing communication, collaboration, support, and appreciation, administrators can build strong relationships with teachers and school staff, leading to improved teaching practices, enhanced student outcomes, and a positive school culture. By working together as a team, administrators, teachers, and school staff can create a nurturing and empowering environment where all members of the school community can thrive and succeed.

Chapter 8: Managing Behavior Challenges

- UNDERSTANDING TRIGGERS and behaviors

Understanding triggers and behaviors is crucial in various contexts, ranging from mental health to addiction recovery. Triggers are external or internal cues that prompt an individual to engage in a particular behavior. These triggers can be anything from a stressful situation to a specific place or person. By recognizing triggers, individuals can better manage their behaviors and prevent harmful responses. Behaviors, on the other hand, are the actions or reactions that result from triggers. Understanding the relationship between triggers and behaviors is essential for developing coping mechanisms and implementing effective interventions.

Triggers can be categorized into several types, including environmental, emotional, social, and physical triggers. Environmental triggers refer to external stimuli, such as loud noises or crowded spaces, that can induce stress or anxiety. Emotional triggers are internal cues linked to specific feelings or memories, like sadness or fear. Social triggers involve interactions with others, such as criticism or rejection, that can provoke negative emotions. Physical triggers pertain to bodily sensations, like pain or hunger, that can influence behavior. Identifying these triggers can help individuals anticipate and mitigate their impact on behavior.

Behaviors are the responses or actions that individuals exhibit in response to triggers. These behaviors can be adaptive or maladaptive, depending on how they help or harm the individual. Adaptive behaviors are healthy coping mechanisms that allow individuals to manage triggers in a constructive manner. These may include deep breathing exercises, mindfulness techniques, or seeking support from loved ones. Maladaptive behaviors, on the other hand, are harmful responses that exacerbate the negative effects of triggers. These may include substance abuse, self-harm, or other destructive behaviors that only mask the underlying issues.

Understanding triggers and behaviors involves recognizing patterns and identifying underlying emotions and thoughts that drive these responses. By developing self-awareness and emotional intelligence, individuals can gain insight into their triggers and behaviors, allowing them to make informed choices and change their responses. Therapy and counseling can be valuable tools in this process, as they provide a supportive environment for individuals to explore their triggers and behaviors in a safe and structured manner. Cognitive-behavioral therapy, in particular, focuses on identifying and challenging irrational beliefs and patterns of thinking that contribute to maladaptive behaviors.

In addiction recovery, understanding triggers and behaviors is essential for maintaining sobriety and preventing relapse. Triggers can be anything from stress or anxiety to social events or negative emotions that prompt cravings for substances. By recognizing these triggers and developing healthy coping mechanisms, individuals in recovery can navigate challenging situations without resorting to substance abuse. Behaviors, such as seeking support from a sponsor or attending therapy sessions, can help individuals cope with triggers in a positive and sustainable way. Building a strong support network and engaging in healthy activities can further reinforce these behaviors and reduce the likelihood of relapse. By identifying and managing triggers, individuals can develop healthier responses and cope with challenges in a constructive manner. Behaviors play a crucial role in this process, as they reflect the ways in which individuals interact with their triggers and environment. Through self-awareness, emotional intelligence, and therapy, individuals can develop coping mechanisms and interventions to address maladaptive behaviors and promote positive change. By taking a proactive and holistic approach to understanding triggers and behaviors, individuals can enhance their overall mental health and quality of life.

- Implementing positive reinforcement and strategies

Positive reinforcement is a valuable tool in behavior management and can be implemented in various settings, including schools, workplaces, and even at home. By rewarding desired behaviors, positive reinforcement encourages individuals to repeat those behaviors in the future. This strategy is effective in shaping behavior because it focuses on promoting positive actions rather than punishing negative ones. In this article, we will explore the benefits of implementing positive reinforcement and discuss strategies for incorporating it into different environments.

One of the key benefits of using positive reinforcement is that it helps to build a positive and supportive environment. When individuals are praised or rewarded for their efforts, they feel valued and appreciated, which can boost their self-esteem and motivation to succeed. This can be particularly beneficial in educational settings, where students may be more likely to engage in learning activities and participate in class when they receive positive feedback. Similarly, in the workplace, employees who are recognized for their hard work are more likely to be productive and satisfied with their jobs. By creating a culture of positivity and encouragement, positive reinforcement can help to improve relationships and overall morale.

In addition to creating a positive environment, positive reinforcement can also be a powerful tool for behavior modification. By rewarding desired behaviors, individuals are more likely to repeat those behaviors in the future. This can be especially useful in changing behaviors that are challenging or undesirable. For example, if a child is struggling to complete their homework, a parent can use positive reinforcement to encourage them to stay focused and complete their assignments. By offering a reward, such as extra playtime or a small treat, the child is motivated to finish their work and may be more willing to do so in the future. This can be a more effective approach than using punishment, which can be demotivating and may not lead to long-term behavior change.

When implementing positive reinforcement, it is important to consider the specific needs and preferences of the individual. Different people may respond to different types of rewards, so it is important to tailor the reinforcement to the individual. For example, while one student may be motivated by verbal praise, another may prefer a small token or sticker. By understanding what motivates each individual, you can create a more effective reinforcement strategy that is tailored to their needs. Additionally, it is important to be consistent in providing reinforcement and to only offer rewards for behaviors that are truly deserving. This helps to reinforce the connection between the behavior and the reward and encourages the individual to continue exhibiting positive behaviors.

In addition to individualizing the reinforcement strategy, it is also important to establish clear and achievable goals. By setting specific objectives for behavior change, individuals have a clear understanding of what is expected of them and can work towards achieving those goals. This helps to provide a sense of structure and direction, which can be motivating for individuals who may be struggling with certain behaviors. For example, if a student is working on improving their attendance in school, setting a goal of attending class for a certain number of consecutive days can help to keep them focused and motivated. By breaking down larger goals into smaller, more manageable tasks, individuals are more likely to be successful in achieving them.

Another key aspect of implementing positive reinforcement is providing immediate feedback. When individuals receive timely and specific feedback on their behaviors, they are better able to understand the connection between their actions and the resulting rewards. This can help to reinforce positive behaviors and encourage individuals to continue exhibiting those behaviors in the future. For example, a teacher who provides immediate praise to a student for participating in class discussions is more likely to see that student continue to engage in class activities. By offering feedback in the moment, individuals are more likely to make the connection between their behaviors and the rewards they receive, which can help to strengthen the reinforcement process. By focusing on rewarding desired behaviors and creating a positive and supportive environment, positive reinforcement can help to motivate individuals to exhibit positive actions and change challenging behaviors. By individualizing the reinforcement strategy, setting clear goals, and providing immediate feedback, individuals are more likely to be successful in achieving behavior change. By incorporating these strategies into different environments, such as schools, workplaces, and homes, positive reinforcement can be a powerful tool for promoting positive behavior and building stronger relationships.

- Seeking help for more complex behaviors

Seeking help for more complex behaviors can be a daunting and overwhelming process for many individuals. When faced with issues such as addiction, bipolar disorder, or personality disorders, it is crucial to reach out for professional support in order to effectively manage and address these complex behaviors. In this article, we will explore the importance of seeking help for more complex behaviors, the different types of professionals who can provide assistance, and the various treatment options available.

One of the key reasons why seeking help for more complex behaviors is essential is because these issues can have a significant impact on an individual's overall well-being and quality of life. Complex behaviors such as addiction or mood disorders can interfere with everyday functioning, relationships, and overall mental health. By seeking professional help, individuals can learn coping mechanisms, develop healthy behaviors, and work towards managing their symptoms in a more effective way. It is important to remember that seeking help is a sign of strength, not weakness, and can lead to positive changes in one's life.

When it comes to seeking help for more complex behaviors, there are a variety of professionals who can provide support and guidance. Psychologists, psychiatrists, counselors, and social workers are just a few examples of professionals who specialize in mental health and can offer assistance to individuals struggling with complex behaviors. Each of these professionals has their own unique set of skills and expertise, which can be tailored to meet the specific needs of the individual seeking help. It is important to research and find a professional who is the right fit for your personal situation and goals.

In addition to seeking help from mental health professionals, there are also a variety of treatment options available for individuals struggling with more complex behaviors. Therapy, medication, support groups, and lifestyle changes are just a few examples of the many options that can be utilized in the treatment of complex behaviors. Therapy, whether individual, group, or family-based, can help individuals understand the root causes of their behaviors, develop coping strategies, and work towards making positive changes in their lives. Medication can also be an effective tool in managing symptoms of complex behaviors, and should be prescribed and monitored by a qualified psychiatrist or physician. Support groups can provide individuals with a sense of community and understanding, while lifestyle changes such as exercise, diet, and stress management can also play a key role in improving mental health.

It is important to remember that seeking help for more complex behaviors is a journey, and progress may not always be linear. Change and growth take time, effort, and patience, and it is important to be kind and understanding towards oneself throughout the process. It is also crucial to have a strong support system in place, whether it be friends, family, or professionals, who can provide encouragement and guidance along the way. By taking the first step towards seeking help, individuals can begin to take control of their lives and work towards a brighter and healthier future. Remember, you are not alone, and help is always available.

Chapter 9: Financial and Legal Considerations

- ACCESSING RESOURCES and funding options

Accessing resources and funding options can be a complex and daunting task for many individuals and organizations. Whether you are a student looking for financial aid to support your education, a small business owner seeking capital to grow your company, or a non-profit organization in need of funding to support your programs, navigating the world of resources and funding can be overwhelming. In this article, we will explore the various options available to individuals and organizations looking to access resources and secure funding for their endeavors.

One of the most common sources of funding for individuals pursuing higher education is financial aid. Financial aid can come in the form of scholarships, grants, loans, or work-study programs. Scholarships are typically awarded based on academic achievement, athletic ability, or other criteria, and do not need to be repaid. Grants are usually awarded based on financial need and also do not need to be repaid. Loans, on the other hand, must be repaid with interest, and work-study programs allow students to work part-time to help cover the cost of their education.

For small business owners, there are a variety of funding options available to help grow and expand their companies. One common option is a small business loan, which can be obtained through traditional banks, credit unions, or online lenders. Small business loans can be used for a variety of purposes, such as purchasing equipment, hiring employees, or expanding operations. Another option for small business owners is to seek out investors, either through venture capital firms or angel investors. These investors provide funding in exchange for a stake in the company, which can help fuel growth and expansion.

Non-profit organizations also have a range of funding options available to support their programs and initiatives. One common source of funding for non-profits is through grants from foundations, corporations, or government agencies. These grants can be used to support specific programs or projects, as well as cover operational expenses. Another funding option for non-profits is through individual donations and fundraising events. Non-profits can also seek out partnerships with businesses or other organizations to secure funding and resources for their initiatives.

In addition to traditional funding sources, there are also alternative options available for accessing resources and funding. Crowdfunding has become a popular way for individuals, businesses, and non-profits to raise money for their endeavors through online platforms. Crowdfunding allows individuals to solicit donations from a large number of people, often in exchange for a reward or incentive. Peer-to-peer lending is another alternative funding option, where individuals can borrow money from other individuals without going through a traditional financial institution.

Ultimately, accessing resources and funding options requires careful research, planning, and determination. It is important to thoroughly explore all funding options available and determine which ones best align with your goals and needs. By being proactive and resourceful, individuals and organizations can successfully secure the resources and funding they need to support their endeavors and achieve their objectives.

- Understanding your rights and entitlements

Understanding your rights and entitlements is crucial in navigating the complex landscape of legal protections and benefits that are available to individuals in various circumstances. These rights and entitlements are designed to uphold the principles of fairness, equality, and justice, ensuring that individuals are treated with respect and dignity in their interactions with others and with institutions. By being knowledgeable about your rights and entitlements, you can assert your position, advocate for yourself, and seek redress if your rights are violated or if you are denied what you are entitled to.

One of the key aspects of understanding your rights and entitlements is knowing where to find information about them. Many resources are available to help individuals learn about their rights, including government websites, legal aid organizations, and advocacy groups. These resources can provide valuable information about the laws and regulations that govern various aspects of life, such as employment, housing, education, healthcare, and civil rights. By familiarizing yourself with the relevant laws and regulations, you can better understand your rights and entitlements in different situations and know how to assert them effectively.

In addition to knowing where to find information about your rights and entitlements, it is important to understand the different types of rights and entitlements that may apply to you. These can include legal rights, such as the right to equal treatment under the law, the right to privacy, and the right to freedom of expression. They can also include social rights, such as the right to education, healthcare, and social security. Understanding the different types of rights and entitlements that you have can help you make informed decisions, seek assistance when needed, and advocate for yourself effectively.

Another important aspect of understanding your rights and entitlements is knowing how to assert them if they are violated or if you are denied what you are entitled to. This may involve taking legal action, seeking assistance from advocacy organizations, or filing complaints with regulatory agencies. By being assertive and proactive in asserting your rights, you can hold others accountable for their actions, seek redress for any harm you have suffered, and prevent future violations of your rights. It is important to remember that you are not alone in asserting your rights and entitlements, as there are many organizations and individuals who can support you in this process. By knowing where to find information about your rights, understanding the different types of rights and entitlements that apply to you, and knowing how to assert them effectively, you can protect yourself from harm, advocate for yourself, and seek redress if your rights are violated. It is important to remember that your rights and entitlements are not just abstract concepts, but tangible protections that can help you lead a dignified and empowered life. By being informed and proactive in asserting your rights, you can ensure that you are treated fairly and justly in all aspects of your life.

- Planning for the future

Planning for the future is a vital aspect of personal and professional development. By setting goals, creating strategies, and anticipating challenges, individuals and organizations can better navigate the uncertainties of the future. In order to effectively plan for the future, it is important to assess current circumstances, identify key priorities, and develop a roadmap for success. This process requires careful consideration of both short-term and long-term objectives, as well as the resources and support needed to achieve them.

One of the first steps in planning for the future is to conduct a thorough analysis of the current situation. This involves taking stock of existing resources, evaluating strengths and weaknesses, and assessing potential opportunities and threats. By understanding where you stand at present, you can better identify areas for improvement and set realistic goals for the future. This assessment should involve input from key stakeholders, including employees, customers, and partners, in order to gain a comprehensive perspective on the current state of affairs.

Once you have a clear understanding of your current situation, the next step is to identify priorities for the future. This involves setting specific, measurable, achievable, relevant, and time-bound (SMART) goals that align with your overall vision and mission. By prioritizing key objectives, you can focus your efforts and resources on the most important areas of improvement. It is important to involve key stakeholders in this process to ensure buy-in and alignment with organizational goals.

In addition to setting goals, it is equally important to develop a strategic plan for achieving them. This involves breaking down long-term objectives into specific action steps, assigning responsibilities, and establishing timelines for completion. By creating a roadmap for success, you can track progress, identify potential roadblocks, and make adjustments as needed. It is important to regularly review and update the strategic plan to ensure that it remains relevant and effective in guiding decision-making and resource allocation.

In planning for the future, it is also essential to anticipate potential challenges and risks. By identifying potential obstacles and developing contingency plans, you can better prepare for unexpected events and disruptions. This involves conducting scenario planning exercises, conducting risk assessments, and developing strategies for mitigating potential threats. By being proactive in addressing challenges, you can better position yourself to navigate uncertainties and achieve your goals.

Ultimately, planning for the future is an ongoing process that requires regular monitoring, assessment, and adjustment. By regularly reviewing progress, analyzing results, and making necessary changes, you can ensure that your plans remain on track and continue to drive success. This involves gathering feedback from key stakeholders, evaluating performance metrics, and making data-driven decisions to guide future actions. By embracing a continuous improvement mindset, you can adapt to changing circumstances and seize new opportunities as they arise. By setting goals, developing strategies, and anticipating challenges, individuals and organizations can better navigate uncertainties and achieve their desired outcomes. By conducting a thorough analysis of the current situation, identifying key priorities, and creating a strategic plan for success, you can position yourself for long-term growth and prosperity. Through proactive monitoring, assessment, and adjustment, you can ensure that your plans remain relevant, effective, and responsive to changing circumstances. By embracing a mindset of continuous improvement, you can adapt to new challenges and opportunities with confidence and resilience.

Chapter 10: Self-Care for Parents

- COPING WITH STRESS and burnout

In today's fast-paced and demanding work environments, stress and burnout have become all too common among employees. Coping with these challenges is essential for maintaining good mental health and overall well-being. Stress is a natural response to pressure or threats, while burnout is a state of emotional, physical, and mental exhaustion caused by excessive and prolonged stress. Both can have serious consequences on an individual's health and performance if not properly managed.

There are several strategies that individuals can use to cope with stress and prevent burnout. One of the most important things is to recognize the signs and symptoms of stress early on. These can manifest themselves in a variety of ways, including irritability, fatigue, headaches, and difficulty concentrating. By being aware of these signs, individuals can take proactive steps to address the underlying causes of stress before it becomes overwhelming.

Another key strategy for coping with stress is to practice self-care. This can involve setting boundaries at work, taking breaks when needed, and prioritizing activities that promote relaxation and well-being. Engaging in regular exercise, getting enough sleep, and maintaining a healthy diet can also help mitigate the effects of stress on the body and mind. Additionally, practicing mindfulness techniques such as meditation or deep breathing can reduce anxiety and improve overall mental health.

Seeking support from friends, family, or a mental health professional is also crucial in coping with stress and burnout. Having a strong support system can provide individuals with the emotional and practical assistance they need to navigate challenging situations. Additionally, talking to a therapist or counselor can help individuals gain perspective on their stressors and develop effective coping strategies. In some cases, medication or other forms of treatment may be necessary to manage severe stress or burnout symptoms.

Creating a healthy work-life balance is another important factor in preventing burnout. This involves setting boundaries between work and personal life, prioritizing activities outside of work that bring joy and relaxation, and learning to delegate tasks when necessary. By maintaining a balance between professional responsibilities and personal well-being, individuals can reduce the risk of burnout and improve their overall quality of life.

Employers also play a crucial role in supporting employees in coping with stress and burnout. Organizations can implement policies and programs that promote work-life balance, provide resources for stress management, and foster a supportive and positive work culture. Additionally, managers can encourage open communication, provide regular feedback and recognition, and offer opportunities for professional development and growth. By creating a supportive work environment, employers can help prevent burnout and improve employee satisfaction and productivity. By recognizing the signs and symptoms of stress, practicing self-care, seeking support, creating a healthy work-life balance, and engaging with supportive employers, individuals can effectively manage stress and prevent burnout. It is important for both individuals and organizations to prioritize mental health and well-being in order to create a positive and healthy work environment for all employees.

- Finding support and community

Finding support and community is essential for overall well-being and mental health. In today's fast-paced world, many individuals are facing increased pressures and stressors in their daily lives. It can be challenging to navigate these challenges on our own, which is why having a support system and a sense of community is so important. By connecting with others who share similar experiences and values, we can feel a sense of belonging and validation that can help us navigate life's ups and downs more successfully.

One of the key benefits of finding support and community is the opportunity to feel understood and validated. When we are facing challenges or going through difficult times, it can be easy to feel isolated and alone. By connecting with others who have experienced similar struggles, we can feel reassured that we are not alone in our experiences. This sense of validation can be incredibly empowering and can help us to build resilience and cope more effectively with our circumstances.

Additionally, finding support and community can provide us with a sense of belonging and connection. Human beings are inherently social creatures, and we thrive when we are able to connect with others in meaningful ways. By forming relationships with like-minded individuals who share our values and interests, we can create a sense of community that can be a source of comfort and support. This sense of belonging can help us to feel more connected to the world around us and can provide us with a sense of purpose and meaning in our lives.

Furthermore, engaging with a supportive community can provide us with valuable resources and information that can help us to navigate life's challenges more effectively. By connecting with others who have been through similar experiences, we can learn from their insights and perspectives and gain valuable knowledge and skills that can help us to overcome our own obstacles. Whether it be through participating in support groups, attending workshops, or engaging in online forums, there are a myriad of ways in which we can access the wisdom and expertise of others who have walked a similar path.

In addition to the practical benefits of finding support and community, there are also emotional and psychological benefits that can greatly enhance our overall well-being. Connecting with others who understand and empathize with our struggles can provide us with a sense of validation and emotional support that can be incredibly healing. When we are able to share our thoughts and feelings with others who listen without judgment, we can experience a profound sense of relief and catharsis that can help us to process our emotions and move forward in a more positive direction.

Moreover, participating in a supportive community can also help us to develop greater self-awareness and self-compassion. By interacting with others who are on a similar journey of personal growth and self-discovery, we can gain valuable insights about ourselves and our patterns of behavior. Through engaging in open and honest dialogue with others, we can gain new perspectives and a deeper understanding of ourselves that can help us to cultivate greater self-acceptance and self-compassion. By connecting with others who share similar experiences and values, we can feel understood, validated, and supported in our journey through life's challenges. In addition to providing practical resources and information, engaging with a supportive community can also offer us emotional and psychological benefits that can help us to cultivate resilience, self-awareness, and self-compassion. Ultimately, by building strong connections with others and fostering a sense of community, we can create a supportive and nurturing environment in which we can thrive and grow.

- Taking care of your own well-being

Taking care of one's own well-being is a fundamental aspect of living a happy and fulfilling life. It encompasses various dimensions such as physical, mental, emotional, and social well-being. In today's fast-paced and hectic world, it is easy to neglect our own needs in favor of work, family, and other responsibilities. However, neglecting our well-being can have serious consequences on our health and overall quality of life.

One of the key aspects of taking care of your own well-being is maintaining a healthy lifestyle. This includes eating a balanced diet, getting regular exercise, and getting enough sleep. Eating a diet rich in fruits, vegetables, and whole grains can provide essential nutrients that support overall health and well-being. Regular exercise not only helps maintain a healthy weight but also boosts mood and energy levels. Getting enough sleep is also crucial for physical and mental health, as it allows the body to rest and recharge.

In addition to physical health, it is important to attend to our mental and emotional well-being. This includes managing stress, finding ways to relax and unwind, and seeking support when needed. Stress can have a detrimental impact on both physical and mental health, so finding healthy ways to cope with stress is essential. This can include activities such as yoga, meditation, or deep breathing exercises. It is also important to make time for activities that bring joy and relaxation, whether it be reading a book, spending time in nature, or engaging in a hobby.

Another important aspect of taking care of your own well-being is nurturing your social connections. Humans are social creatures, and having strong social connections can have a positive impact on mental and emotional well-being. This can include spending time with friends and family, joining social groups or clubs, or volunteering in the community. Building and maintaining these connections can provide a sense of belonging, support, and fulfillment.

Self-care is also an important part of maintaining well-being. This includes setting boundaries, saying no when necessary, and prioritizing your own needs. It can be easy to put others' needs before our own, but neglecting our own well-being can lead to burnout and resentment. Learning to prioritize self-care and set boundaries can help ensure that we are able to meet our own needs and prevent feelings of overwhelm or exhaustion. By prioritizing physical, mental, emotional, and social well-being, we can improve our overall quality of life and ensure that we are able to meet the demands of everyday life. This may involve making small changes to our daily habits, setting boundaries, and finding ways to relax and unwind. By taking the time to care for ourselves, we can better support our health and well-being in the long run.

Chapter 11: Celebrating Milestones and Achievements

- RECOGNIZING PROGRESS and growth

Recognizing progress and growth is an essential aspect of personal and professional development. It is important to acknowledge and celebrate the milestones and achievements that we have accomplished along the way. By recognizing progress and growth, we can cultivate a sense of motivation and encouragement to continue moving forward towards our goals.

One way to recognize progress and growth is to set clear and achievable goals. By establishing specific objectives, we can track our progress and see how far we have come. When we reach a goal or milestone, it is important to take a moment to celebrate and acknowledge the hard work and effort that went into achieving it. This can help reinforce positive behaviors and foster a sense of accomplishment.

Another important aspect of recognizing progress and growth is to practice self-reflection. By taking the time to reflect on our actions and decisions, we can gain valuable insights into our strengths and weaknesses. This self-awareness can help us identify areas for improvement and set new goals for personal and professional growth. Reflecting on our progress can also help us appreciate how much we have learned and grown over time.

Feedback from others is another valuable tool for recognizing progress and growth. Seeking feedback from colleagues, mentors, and friends can provide valuable insights into how others perceive our progress and can help us identify blind spots or areas for improvement. Constructive feedback can also serve as a source of motivation and encouragement to keep pushing forward towards our goals.

It is important to remember that progress and growth are not always linear. There may be setbacks and challenges along the way, but it is important to see these as opportunities for learning and growth. Embracing failure as a natural part of the growth process can help us develop resilience and perseverance in the face of obstacles. By setting clear goals, practicing self-reflection, seeking feedback, and embracing failure, we can cultivate a growth mindset that will enable us to continue moving forward towards our goals. Celebrating our achievements and milestones along the way can fuel our motivation and drive to strive for even greater success in the future.

- Setting goals and objectives

Setting goals and objectives is a crucial aspect of personal and professional development. Goals provide a sense of direction and purpose, while objectives serve as the stepping stones to achieving those goals. By clearly defining what you want to achieve and breaking it down into smaller, manageable tasks, you can increase your motivation, focus, and productivity. Whether you are pursuing a new career path, starting a business, or striving to improve your health and well-being, setting clear goals and objectives is key to success.

When setting goals, it is important to make them specific, measurable, attainable, relevant, and time-bound. This is often referred to as the SMART criteria. By creating goals that are specific, you can clearly define what you want to achieve and how you will measure your progress. Making goals measurable allows you to track your success and adjust your plans as needed. Setting attainable goals ensures that they are within reach and realistic given your resources and abilities. Making goals relevant to your values and priorities will increase your motivation to achieve them. To bring to a close, setting time-bound goals gives you a deadline to work towards, creating a sense of urgency and focus.

Objectives are the actionable steps you need to take to achieve your goals. They are specific, measurable, and time-bound tasks that move you closer to your ultimate objective. By breaking down your larger goals into smaller objectives, you can create a roadmap for success. For example, if your goal is to start a new business, your objectives might include conducting market research, creating a business plan, securing funding, and launching your product or service. By setting clear objectives and tracking your progress, you can stay on course and make adjustments as needed to reach your ultimate goal.

In order to set effective goals and objectives, it is important to first identify what you truly want to achieve. This involves reflecting on your values, priorities, strengths, and limitations. By understanding your motivations and aspirations, you can set goals that are meaningful and inspiring. It is also helpful to consider your current situation and resources, as well as any potential obstacles or challenges you may face along the way. By taking a realistic and introspective approach to goal-setting, you can increase your chances of success and avoid setting yourself up for failure.

Once you have identified your goals, it is important to write them down and create a plan of action. Writing down your goals makes them tangible and concrete, and will help keep you accountable. Your plan of action should outline the steps you need to take to achieve your goals, as well as any potential obstacles or challenges you may encounter. It can be helpful to break down your plan into smaller tasks and set deadlines for each one. By creating a roadmap for success, you can stay organized, focused, and motivated as you work towards your goals.

It is also important to regularly monitor and evaluate your progress towards your goals and objectives. This involves tracking your performance, adjusting your strategies as needed, and celebrating your successes along the way. By regularly assessing your progress, you can stay on track and make any necessary adjustments to ensure that you are moving closer towards your goals. It can be helpful to set regular check-in points to review your progress and make any necessary changes to your plan of action. By staying flexible and adaptable, you can increase your chances of success and overcome any obstacles that may arise. By creating clear, specific, and measurable goals, and breaking them down into actionable objectives, you can increase your motivation, focus, and productivity. By aligning your goals with your values and priorities, and creating a realistic plan of action, you can increase your chances of success and achieve your desired outcomes. By regularly monitoring and evaluating your progress, and making adjustments as needed, you can stay on course and achieve your goals. Setting goals and objectives is a powerful tool for personal growth and achievement, and can help you reach your full potential.

- Empowering your child for the future

Empowering your child for the future is a critical aspect of parenting in today's rapidly changing world. As parents, we have a responsibility to equip our children with the necessary skills, knowledge, and values to succeed in tomorrow's society. This means going beyond just providing for their basic needs and ensuring they have a strong foundation for personal and professional growth. By taking an active role in our children's development, we can help them build resilience, adaptability, and a growth mindset that will serve them well in the face of challenges and opportunities.

One of the key ways to empower your child for the future is to encourage them to be curious and independent learners. This means fostering a love of learning, a sense of wonder, and a willingness to take risks and explore new ideas. By instilling a growth mindset in our children, we can help them see challenges as opportunities for growth and development rather than setbacks. Encouraging them to ask questions, seek out information, and think critically will set them up for success in school, in their careers, and in life.

In addition to promoting a love of learning, it is important to teach our children valuable life skills that will serve them well in the future. This includes teaching them how to manage their time effectively, set goals, and prioritize tasks. By instilling these skills early on, we can help our children develop a sense of agency and autonomy that will serve them well as they navigate the complexities of adulthood. Teaching them financial literacy, emotional intelligence, and social skills will also help them build strong relationships, make sound decisions, and navigate the ups and downs of life with confidence and resilience.

Furthermore, it is important to nurture our children's creativity and problem-solving skills. In a world that is increasingly driven by innovation and technology, the ability to think outside the box and come up with creative solutions to complex problems is more important than ever. By encouraging our children to explore their interests, experiment with different ideas, and take risks, we can help them develop the creativity and resilience needed to thrive in a rapidly changing world. Providing them with opportunities to engage in hands-on, experiential learning experiences will also help them develop the critical thinking skills and confidence needed to tackle the challenges of the future.

Another key aspect of empowering your child for the future is teaching them the importance of empathy, compassion, and social responsibility. In a world that is becoming increasingly interconnected, it is essential for our children to understand the impact of their actions on others and to develop a sense of social responsibility. By teaching them the value of kindness, compassion, and respect for others, we can help them become empathetic and inclusive individuals who are attuned to the needs and perspectives of others. This will not only help them build strong relationships and navigate social situations with ease but also contribute to a more just and equitable society. By fostering a love of learning, teaching valuable life skills, nurturing creativity and problem-solving skills, and promoting empathy and social responsibility, we can help our children thrive in a rapidly changing world. As parents, we have a unique opportunity to shape the next generation of leaders, thinkers, and changemakers who will have a positive impact on the world around them. By investing in our children's growth and development, we can help them realize their full potential and navigate the complexities of the future with confidence, resilience, and a sense of purpose.

Chapter 12: Siblings and Family Support

- SUPPORTING SIBLINGS of children with autism

Supporting siblings of children with autism is a critical aspect of ensuring the overall well-being and development of the entire family unit. Siblings of children with autism face unique challenges that can impact their emotional, social, and psychological well-being. These challenges can include feelings of neglect, resentment, frustration, isolation, and even guilt. It is important for parents, caregivers, and professionals to recognize the needs of siblings and provide them with the support and resources they need to thrive.

One of the key ways to support siblings of children with autism is through open communication and education. It is important for parents and caregivers to have honest and age-appropriate conversations with siblings about their sibling's autism diagnosis and what it means for the family. Providing siblings with information about autism and helping them understand their sibling's unique needs can help reduce feelings of confusion and resentment. Additionally, educating siblings about autism can foster empathy and understanding, creating a more supportive and inclusive family environment.

In addition to education, creating a sense of routine and structure can be beneficial for siblings of children with autism. Children thrive on predictability and consistency, and this is especially important for siblings who may feel overwhelmed by the unpredictable nature of their sibling's behavior. Establishing a daily routine that includes time for individual activities, family time, and support for the child with autism can help siblings feel more secure and balanced. Consistent routines can also provide siblings with a sense of control and agency in their daily lives.

Moreover, providing siblings with opportunities for one-on-one time with parents or caregivers can help strengthen the bond between siblings and ensure they feel valued and important within the family unit. Siblings of children with autism may often feel overlooked or overshadowed by their sibling's needs, so it is important to carve out special time for them to express their thoughts, feelings, and concerns. This individualized attention can also help siblings feel supported and connected to their parents, fostering a sense of security and love within the family.

Another important aspect of supporting siblings of children with autism is connecting them with external support networks and resources. Siblings of children with autism may benefit from participating in support groups or therapy sessions specifically designed for siblings of individuals with autism. These resources can provide siblings with a safe space to express their emotions, share their experiences, and connect with others who understand their unique challenges. Additionally, connecting siblings with mentors or other positive role models who have experience with autism can help siblings feel less alone and more empowered to navigate their feelings and experiences.

Furthermore, promoting open communication and collaboration within the family unit is essential for supporting siblings of children with autism. Parents, caregivers, and siblings should feel comfortable expressing their thoughts, concerns, and needs with one another in a respectful and empathetic manner. Creating a family environment where everyone's voice is heard and valued can help siblings feel supported and validated in their experiences. Additionally, involving siblings in decision-making processes regarding their sibling's care and treatment can help them feel more involved and invested in their sibling's well-being.

Ultimately, supporting siblings of children with autism requires a holistic approach that takes into account their unique needs, challenges, and experiences. By providing siblings with education, routine, one-on-one time, external resources, and open communication, parents, caregivers, and professionals can help siblings thrive and develop a strong sense of resilience, empathy, and understanding. It is crucial for families to prioritize the well-being of all members, including siblings, in order to create a supportive and nurturing environment for everyone to flourish.

- Maintaining balance and harmony in the family

Maintaining balance and harmony in the family is a key aspect of creating a healthy and thriving household. Family dynamics are complex and can be influenced by a variety of factors, including individual personalities, communication styles, and external stressors. In order to foster a positive family environment, it is important for all members to work together to establish clear boundaries, communicate effectively, and prioritize quality time spent together.

One of the first steps in maintaining balance and harmony in the family is setting boundaries and expectations. Each family member should be able to voice their needs and preferences in a respectful manner, and all parties should be willing to compromise in order to find common ground. By establishing clear boundaries, such as designated quiet times for studying or work, and expectations, such as completing household chores in a timely manner, families can avoid misunderstandings and conflicts that can disrupt the harmony of the household.

Effective communication is essential for maintaining balance and harmony in the family. Families that are able to openly discuss their thoughts, feelings, and concerns are better equipped to resolve conflicts and build strong relationships. Active listening, empathy, and nonverbal communication can all play important roles in fostering healthy communication within the family. By creating a safe space for open dialogue and respecting each other's perspectives, family members can work together to address issues and find solutions that benefit everyone.

Quality time spent together is another important factor in maintaining balance and harmony in the family. In today's fast-paced world, it can be easy for family members to become disconnected and overwhelmed by their individual responsibilities. By prioritizing quality time spent together, families can strengthen their bonds, create positive memories, and reinforce their sense of unity. Whether it's through shared meals, family outings, or game nights, finding opportunities to connect and have fun together can help families maintain a sense of balance and harmony.

In addition to setting boundaries, communicating effectively, and spending quality time together, families can also maintain balance and harmony by practicing self-care and prioritizing individual well-being. When family members take care of themselves physically, mentally, and emotionally, they are better equipped to handle the challenges and stresses of daily life. By setting clear boundaries, communicating effectively, spending quality time together, practicing self-care, and prioritizing individual well-being, families can create a positive and harmonious household where each member feels valued, supported, and respected. By working together to address conflicts, celebrate successes, and support each other through life's ups and downs, families can create a strong foundation for a happy and fulfilling life together.

- Building a strong support network

Building a strong support network is essential for success in both personal and professional endeavors. A support network consists of friends, family members, colleagues, mentors, and other individuals who provide emotional support, practical assistance, and guidance when needed. This network can play a crucial role in helping individuals navigate challenges, reach their goals, and maintain overall well-being. In this article, we will explore the importance of building a strong support network, discuss strategies for cultivating and sustaining meaningful relationships, and offer tips for maximizing the benefits of your support system.

One of the key benefits of having a strong support network is the emotional support it provides during difficult times. Life can be unpredictable and challenging, and having a group of people who care about you and are willing to listen and offer encouragement can make all the difference. Whether you are going through a breakup, dealing with a health issue, facing a work-related problem, or simply feeling overwhelmed, having a support network to turn to can help you cope with stress and build resilience. Studies have shown that social support is associated with better mental health outcomes, including lower levels of depression and anxiety. By nurturing relationships with individuals who make you feel valued and supported, you can improve your emotional well-being and boost your overall quality of life.

In addition to providing emotional support, a strong support network can also offer practical assistance and resources. Your network can help you brainstorm solutions to problems, offer guidance and advice based on their own experiences, provide referrals to useful services or professionals, and even assist you with tasks or projects. For example, if you are starting a new business, your support network may include individuals who have expertise in entrepreneurship and can offer valuable insights and connections. If you are struggling with a particular skill or subject, you may have friends or colleagues who can provide tutoring or mentoring. By leveraging the diverse strengths and resources of your support network, you can access a wealth of knowledge and expertise that can help you overcome obstacles and achieve your goals.

Another important benefit of building a strong support network is the sense of belonging and connectedness it can offer. Human beings are social creatures, and we thrive on connection with others. Having a support network can provide a sense of community and belonging that can enhance your sense of purpose and fulfillment. When you know that you have people in your corner who care about you and are invested in your success, you are more likely to feel confident and motivated to pursue your aspirations. In times of celebration, your support network can share in your joy and make your achievements even sweeter. And in times of sorrow, they can lend a listening ear and a shoulder to lean on. By cultivating meaningful relationships with others, you can cultivate a sense of connection and belonging that can enrich your life in countless ways.

Building a strong support network requires intentional effort and commitment. Like any relationship, meaningful connections take time to develop and nurture. It is important to invest in your relationships by showing genuine interest, empathy, and support for the people in your network. This may involve regular communication, active listening, and reciprocity in terms of offering help and being receptive to feedback. It is also important to be authentic and vulnerable in your interactions, as this can deepen trust and intimacy with others. Building a support network is a two-way street, so it is essential to be willing to give as well as receive support from others. By being a reliable and supportive presence in the lives of your network members, you can strengthen your relationships and create a mutually beneficial support system.

There are several strategies you can use to cultivate and maintain a strong support network. One of the first steps is to identify the people in your life who are already part of your network, as well as those you would like to add. Think about the individuals who make you feel supported, understood, and valued, and make an effort to deepen those relationships. Consider reaching out to old friends, colleagues, or acquaintances who you haven't connected with in a while, as well as seeking out new connections through networking events, social gatherings, or online communities. It can also be helpful to join groups or organizations that align with your interests or values, as these can be great sources of potential support and connection. By expanding your social circle and diversifying your network, you can increase the likelihood of finding individuals who can offer different perspectives, expertise, and resources.

Once you have identified potential members of your support network, it is important to nurture those relationships through regular and meaningful interactions. This can involve scheduling one-on-one meetings, attending group outings or events, or participating in shared hobbies or activities. It is also important to communicate openly and honestly with your network members, expressing your needs, boundaries, and expectations in a clear and respectful manner. By setting healthy boundaries and establishing clear guidelines for communication and support, you can minimize misunderstandings and conflicts while fostering trust and accountability within your network. It is also important to show appreciation for the people in your support network, acknowledging their contributions and expressing gratitude for their presence in your life. By cultivating a culture of gratitude and reciprocity within your network, you can strengthen the bonds of trust and connection that hold your support system together.

In addition to nurturing existing relationships, it is important to continually seek out new connections and opportunities for growth within your support network. This can involve expanding your social circle, seeking out mentors or advisors who can offer guidance and support, or participating in group activities or events that align with your interests and goals. It is also important to be open to feedback and constructive criticism from your network members, as this can help you identify areas for improvement and growth. By being willing to learn from others and adapt to new perspectives, you can strengthen your relationships and expand your support system in meaningful ways. Building a strong support network is an ongoing process that requires dedication, effort, and vulnerability. By investing in your relationships and being intentional about cultivating meaningful connections, you can create a support system that enhances your well-being, resilience, and success in all areas of life.

Chapter 13: Teenage Years and Transitioning to Adulthood

- PREPARING FOR ADOLESCENCE and independence

Preparing for adolescence and independence is a critical period in a young person's life that requires careful consideration and planning. Adolescence is a time of significant change and growth, both physically and emotionally. It is a time when young people are transitioning from childhood to adulthood, and it is essential to help them navigate this period with support and guidance. Independence is a crucial aspect of adolescence, as it is during this time that young people begin to assert their autonomy and develop their own identity.

One of the most important ways to prepare for adolescence and independence is to establish clear and open communication channels with young people. Adolescents are going through a period of intense change, and it is essential for parents, caregivers, and educators to listen to their concerns and provide guidance and support. By creating an environment where young people feel comfortable expressing themselves, we can help them navigate the challenges of adolescence with confidence and resilience.

In addition to open communication, it is important to provide young people with the tools they need to succeed in adolescence and independence. This includes teaching them important life skills such as time management, decision-making, and conflict resolution. By empowering young people with these skills, we can help them become more independent and capable of navigating the challenges of adolescence.

It is also important to set clear boundaries and expectations for young people during adolescence. While it is important to give young people autonomy and independence, it is also essential to establish guidelines and rules to help them make responsible decisions. By setting clear boundaries, we can help young people understand the importance of accountability and self-discipline.

Another important aspect of preparing for adolescence and independence is to foster a sense of self-esteem and self-confidence in young people. Adolescence can be a challenging time, and young people may face issues such as peer pressure, body image concerns, and academic stress. By helping young people develop a strong sense of self-worth and confidence, we can help them navigate these challenges with resilience and determination.

It is also important to help young people develop healthy relationships with peers and adults. Adolescence is a time when young people are seeking to establish their identities and form connections with others. By nurturing positive relationships with peers and adults, we can help young people develop important social skills and emotional intelligence that will serve them well in adolescence and beyond.

Ultimately, it is important to encourage young people to explore their interests and passions during adolescence. Adolescence is a time of self-discovery, and young people may have a variety of interests and talents that they want to pursue. By providing opportunities for young people to explore their interests and passions, we can help them develop a sense of purpose and direction that will guide them through adolescence and into adulthood. By establishing clear communication channels, providing young people with essential life skills, setting boundaries and expectations, fostering self-esteem and confidence, nurturing healthy relationships, and encouraging exploration of interests and passions, we can help young people navigate the challenges of adolescence with confidence and resilience. By taking a proactive and supportive approach to preparing young people for adolescence and independence, we can help them develop the skills and resilience they need to succeed in adulthood.

- Exploring options for further education and employment

When considering options for further education and employment, it is important to carefully evaluate your interests, skills, and long-term goals. There are a variety of pathways available to individuals seeking to advance their careers or acquire new skills, ranging from traditional degrees in a specific field to vocational training programs that focus on practical skills.

One of the most common options for further education is pursuing a higher degree, such as a master's or doctoral degree. These programs are typically more specialized and in-depth than undergraduate degrees, allowing students to develop a deeper understanding of their chosen field. In addition, earning a higher degree can increase job opportunities and potential for higher salaries in many fields.

Another option for further education is enrolling in a vocational training program. These programs are often shorter in duration than traditional college degrees and focus on developing practical skills that are directly applicable to specific industries or occupations. Vocational training programs are ideal for individuals who are looking to quickly gain the necessary skills to enter a new career field or advance in their current field.

In addition to traditional higher education and vocational training programs, another option for further education is online learning. Online courses and degree programs have become increasingly popular in recent years, allowing individuals to pursue further education on their own schedule and from the comfort of their own home. Online learning is a great option for individuals who may have other commitments, such as a full-time job or family responsibilities, that make attending traditional classes difficult.

When exploring options for further education, it is important to consider your long-term career goals and how each option aligns with those goals. For example, if you are looking to advance in a specific field, it may be beneficial to pursue a higher degree in that field to gain a deeper understanding and increase your job prospects. On the other hand, if you are looking to quickly gain new skills for a specific job or industry, a vocational training program may be the best option for you.

When it comes to employment options, there are a variety of factors to consider, including job market trends, salary potential, and job satisfaction. It is important to research potential employers and industries to determine where there may be opportunities for growth and advancement. Networking with professionals in your desired field can also be beneficial in gaining insight into potential job opportunities and career paths.

Ultimately, the key to exploring options for further education and employment is to carefully evaluate your interests, skills, and long-term goals. By taking the time to research and consider all of the available options, you can make an informed decision that will set you on the path to success in your chosen career field. Whether you choose to pursue a higher degree, enroll in a vocational training program, or explore online learning, investing in your education and career development is a valuable investment in your future.

- Planning for long-term support

Planning for long-term support is an essential part of ensuring that individuals with disabilities or chronic health conditions have the resources and assistance they need to live fulfilling and independent lives. Long-term support encompasses a range of services and supports that help individuals with disabilities maintain their quality of life and participate fully in their communities. This includes personal care services, respite care, transportation assistance, assistive technology, and specialized therapies. By creating a comprehensive long-term support plan, individuals can anticipate their future needs and access the necessary services to support their goals and aspirations.

One of the key aspects of planning for long-term support is starting early and building a strong support network. Individuals should begin thinking about their long-term care needs well in advance, ideally in their 20s or 30s. By starting early, individuals can proactively address any current or potential health issues, set long-term goals, and establish a support network of family, friends, healthcare providers, and community resources. Developing a strong support network is crucial for navigating the complex world of long-term care services and ensuring that individuals receive the best possible care and support.

Another important consideration when planning for long-term support is identifying the available resources and funding options. Long-term care services can be costly, and individuals need to explore all possible funding sources to ensure they can access the care they need. This may include private insurance, government-funded programs like Medicaid or Medicare, and personal savings or assets. It is important for individuals to thoroughly research and understand their options for funding long-term care services, as different programs have different eligibility criteria and coverage limits.

In addition to identifying funding sources, individuals should also consider the range of long-term care options available to them. There are a variety of long-term care settings, including nursing homes, assisted living facilities, in-home care services, and community-based programs. Each setting offers different levels of care and support, and individuals should carefully consider their specific needs and preferences when choosing a long-term care option. It is important to explore all available options and consult with healthcare providers and support networks to make an informed decision about the best care setting for individual needs.

Another important aspect of planning for long-term support is creating a comprehensive care plan that addresses all aspects of an individual's physical, emotional, and social well-being. A care plan should be tailored to an individual's unique needs and goals, taking into account their strengths, preferences, and limitations. This can include medical management, therapy services, mobility aids, social activities, and emotional support. By creating a holistic care plan that addresses all aspects of an individual's well-being, individuals can maximize their quality of life and maintain their independence for as long as possible.

To conclude, it is crucial for individuals to regularly review and update their long-term support plans as their needs and circumstances change. Life is unpredictable, and individuals may experience changes in their health, relationships, or financial situation that necessitate adjustments to their care plan. By regularly reviewing and updating their long-term support plans, individuals can ensure that they are receiving the most appropriate care and support to meet their evolving needs. This may include reassessing funding options, exploring new care settings, or adjusting goals and priorities based on changing circumstances. By starting early, building a strong support network, identifying funding sources, exploring care options, creating a comprehensive care plan, and regularly reviewing and updating their plans, individuals can proactively address their long-term care needs and maximize their quality of life. With careful planning and preparation, individuals can navigate the complexities of long-term care services and receive the support they need to thrive.

Chapter 14: Cultivating Independence and Life Skills

- TEACHING DAILY LIVING skills

Teaching daily living skills is a vital aspect of education that is often overlooked in traditional academic settings. These skills are essential for individuals to navigate and function independently in their daily lives. From personal hygiene and meal preparation to household chores and time management, daily living skills encompass a wide range of activities that are necessary for personal well-being and success. By teaching these skills, educators can empower students to become more self-sufficient and capable of taking care of themselves in various life situations. By acquiring these skills, individuals are better equipped to handle the challenges and responsibilities that come with daily living, leading to increased confidence and self-esteem. In addition, mastering daily living skills can also improve social interactions and relationships, as individuals are more likely to feel comfortable and confident in various social settings.

Furthermore, teaching daily living skills is crucial for promoting autonomy and personal growth in individuals. By empowering individuals to take charge of their own lives and make informed decisions about their daily routines, educators can help them develop a sense of agency and self-efficacy. This sense of empowerment is essential for individuals to navigate the complexities of modern life and overcome obstacles that may arise. By acquiring daily living skills, individuals are better prepared to face challenges and adapt to changing circumstances, leading to increased resilience and adaptability in the face of adversity.

Additionally, teaching daily living skills can have a positive impact on academic performance and success. Research has shown that individuals who possess strong daily living skills are better able to manage their time effectively, maintain healthy routines, and balance various responsibilities in their lives. These skills are essential for academic success, as they enable individuals to stay organized, focused, and motivated in their studies. By integrating daily living skills into the curriculum, educators can help students develop the habits and routines that are necessary for academic achievement and success. By acquiring these skills, individuals are better prepared to navigate the complexities of daily life and overcome challenges that may arise. Additionally, mastering daily living skills can have a positive impact on academic performance and success, as it enables individuals to stay organized, focused, and motivated in their studies.

- Fostering independence and autonomy

Fostering independence and autonomy is a crucial aspect of personal development and growth, particularly in the field of education. Many educators and researchers believe that promoting independence in students can lead to greater success in both academic and personal endeavors. Independence is defined as the ability to make decisions and take actions on one's own, without relying on others for guidance or approval. Autonomy, on the other hand, refers to the ability to govern oneself and make independent choices based on one's own values and beliefs.

There are numerous benefits to fostering independence and autonomy in students. Firstly, independent and autonomous individuals are better equipped to handle the challenges and responsibilities of adulthood. By developing the skills necessary to make decisions and solve problems on their own, students are better prepared to navigate the complexities of the real world. Additionally, fostering independence and autonomy can lead to increased motivation and self-esteem. When students are given the opportunity to take ownership of their learning and make choices about their education, they are more likely to feel empowered and motivated to succeed.

There are several strategies that educators can use to promote independence and autonomy in their students. One effective approach is to provide students with opportunities for self-directed learning. This could involve encouraging students to set their own goals, create their own study plans, and pursue topics that interest them. By giving students more control over their learning, educators can help them develop the skills necessary to take ownership of their education.

Another strategy is to provide students with opportunities for decision-making and problem-solving. This could involve assigning group projects or tasks that require students to work together to find solutions. By engaging in collaborative activities, students can learn to communicate effectively, negotiate with others, and make decisions as a team. These experiences can help students develop the critical thinking and problem-solving skills necessary to become independent and autonomous learners.

It is also important for educators to provide students with constructive feedback and support as they work towards becoming more independent and autonomous. By offering praise for their efforts and guidance on how to improve, educators can help students build confidence in their abilities and develop a growth mindset. Additionally, educators can model independence and autonomy in their own actions and decisions. By demonstrating these qualities in their own behavior, educators can inspire students to take control of their own learning and development. By promoting independence, educators can help students develop the skills and mindset necessary to thrive in the real world. By providing students with opportunities for self-directed learning, decision-making, and problem-solving, educators can empower them to take ownership of their education and make informed choices about their future. Ultimately, fostering independence and autonomy in students is about giving them the tools they need to become resilient, self-reliant, and confident individuals who are capable of tackling any challenge that comes their way.

- Preparing your child for life beyond the home

Preparing your child for life beyond the home is a crucial task that requires careful planning and consideration. As a parent, it is essential to equip your child with the necessary skills and knowledge to succeed in the ever-changing world outside the comfort of home. This includes teaching them important life skills such as financial literacy, time management, problem-solving, and interpersonal communication. By instilling these skills early on, you can help your child build a solid foundation for success and independence in the future.

One of the most important aspects of preparing your child for life beyond the home is teaching them financial literacy. This includes teaching them the basics of budgeting, saving, and managing money responsibly. By teaching your child the value of money and how to make wise financial decisions, you can help them avoid financial pitfalls and set them on the path to financial stability and success. With the rise of online banking and digital payment methods, it is also important to teach your child how to manage their finances in a digital world. This includes teaching them how to create and stick to a budget, track their expenses, and save for the future.

In addition to financial literacy, it is also important to teach your child the importance of time management. Time management is a crucial skill that can help your child excel in both academics and their future career. By teaching your child how to prioritize tasks, set goals, and manage their time effectively, you can help them become more organized and productive individuals. This includes teaching them how to create to-do lists, prioritize tasks, and balance their academic, extracurricular, and social commitments. By instilling good time management habits early on, you can help your child develop the skills they need to succeed in the fast-paced and demanding world outside the home.

Another important skill to teach your child is problem-solving. Life is full of challenges and obstacles, and it is important for your child to be able to navigate these challenges effectively. By teaching your child how to think critically, analyze problems, and come up with creative solutions, you can help them develop the problem-solving skills they need to overcome obstacles and achieve their goals. This includes encouraging your child to think outside the box, explore different perspectives, and collaborate with others to find solutions. By teaching your child how to approach problems with a positive and proactive mindset, you can help them become resilient and adaptable individuals who are ready to face any challenge that comes their way.

In brief, it is important to teach your child the importance of interpersonal communication. Effective communication skills are essential for success in all aspects of life, from building strong relationships to advancing in a career. By teaching your child how to express themselves clearly, listen actively, and communicate effectively with others, you can help them develop the interpersonal skills they need to thrive in social settings and professional environments. This includes teaching your child how to communicate confidently, assertively, and respectfully, both in person and through digital channels. By cultivating strong communication skills in your child, you can help them build strong relationships, collaborate effectively with others, and succeed in a diverse and interconnected world. By teaching your child important life skills such as financial literacy, time management, problem-solving, and interpersonal communication, you can help them build a solid foundation for success and independence in the future. By instilling these skills early on and providing them with the support and guidance they need, you can help your child navigate the challenges of the ever-changing world outside the home with confidence and resilience. Remember, as a parent, you play a crucial role in shaping your child's future, and by investing in their growth and development, you can help them reach their full potential and thrive in all aspects of life.

Chapter 15: Connecting with the Autistic Community

- FINDING ACCEPTANCE and understanding

Finding acceptance and understanding is a crucial aspect of human interactions and relationships. In our daily lives, we encounter situations where we may feel misunderstood or judged by others. This can lead to feelings of isolation, loneliness, and resentment. However, by seeking acceptance and understanding, we can foster more meaningful and fulfilling connections with others.

Acceptance is the act of recognizing and embracing someone for who they are, without trying to change or judge them. It involves acknowledging their thoughts, feelings, and experiences, even if they may differ from our own. Acceptance is a powerful tool in building trust and rapport with others, as it demonstrates a willingness to listen and empathize with their perspective. When we accept others unconditionally, we create a safe and welcoming space for authentic communication and genuine connection.

Understanding, on the other hand, is the ability to comprehend someone else's point of view and empathize with their emotions and experiences. It requires active listening, open-mindedness, and a genuine curiosity to learn about another person's thoughts and feelings. By seeking to understand others, we demonstrate respect and compassion, which can help bridge the gap between different perspectives and foster mutual respect and cooperation.

In order to find acceptance and understanding in our relationships, it is important to cultivate qualities such as patience, empathy, and humility. Patience allows us to listen attentively to others, without rushing to judgment or giving in to impulsive reactions. Empathy enables us to put ourselves in someone else's shoes and see the world from their perspective, which can help us connect on a deeper level and forge stronger bonds. Humility reminds us that we are not always right and that we can learn and grow from others' insights and experiences.

One of the key factors in finding acceptance and understanding is effective communication. By expressing our thoughts, feelings, and needs clearly and respectfully, we can create a shared understanding with others and avoid misunderstandings and conflicts. Active listening is also crucial in fostering acceptance and understanding, as it shows that we value and respect the other person's perspective and are willing to engage in a meaningful dialogue.

It is also important to practice self-acceptance and self-understanding in order to cultivate acceptance and understanding in our relationships with others. By acknowledging and embracing our own flaws and imperfections, we can develop greater compassion and empathy for the struggles and challenges of others. Self-awareness allows us to recognize our own biases, judgments, and limitations, and work towards overcoming them in order to connect more deeply with those around us. By cultivating acceptance and understanding in our relationships, we can create a more harmonious and connected world, where differences are celebrated and all voices are heard and respected. It is through openness, empathy, and self-awareness that we can truly connect with others and find the acceptance and understanding we seek in our interactions and relationships.

- Building relationships within the autism community

Building relationships within the autism community is an essential aspect of creating a supportive and inclusive environment for individuals with autism spectrum disorder (ASD). The autism community is comprised of individuals with ASD, their families, caregivers, teachers, therapists, advocates, researchers, and other professionals who work with individuals on the spectrum. It is a diverse and complex community that requires collaboration, understanding, and empathy to effectively support individuals with ASD in reaching their full potential.

One of the key principles of building relationships within the autism community is fostering a sense of acceptance and inclusion for individuals with

ASD. This means recognizing and valuing the unique strengths and abilities of individuals on the spectrum, as well as respecting their differences and challenges. By creating a welcoming and supportive environment, individuals with ASD can feel more comfortable and confident in expressing themselves and engaging with others. This can help to build trust and rapport between individuals with ASD and others in the community, leading to more positive and meaningful relationships.

Communication is another essential factor in building relationships within the autism community. Effective communication involves listening actively, being open-minded, and being sensitive to the needs and preferences of individuals with ASD. It is important to communicate clearly and directly, using language and methods that are accessible and understandable to individuals on the spectrum. By creating a safe and supportive space for communication, individuals with ASD can feel more empowered to express their thoughts, feelings, and needs, and to engage in meaningful interactions with others.

Collaboration is also key to building relationships within the autism community. Collaboration involves working together with individuals with ASD, their families, caregivers, and other stakeholders to identify and address the needs and priorities of the community. By collaborating on projects, programs, and initiatives, members of the autism community can pool their resources, expertise, and perspectives to achieve common goals and outcomes. Collaboration can also help to foster a sense of unity, connection, and shared purpose among individuals with ASD and others in the community.

Building relationships within the autism community also involves promoting awareness and education about ASD and related issues. By raising awareness about autism and providing education and training to individuals, families, caregivers, and professionals, we can increase understanding, reduce stigma, and promote acceptance and inclusion for individuals with ASD. By sharing information, resources, and best practices, we can help to build a more informed and supportive community that is better equipped to meet the needs of individuals with ASD. By fostering acceptance, communication, collaboration, and awareness, we can create a more supportive and inclusive community that empowers individuals with ASD to thrive and succeed. By working together, we can build a stronger and more connected autism community that is better able to advocate for the rights and needs of individuals on the spectrum. Together, we can create a brighter future for individuals with ASD and their families.

- Advocating for autism awareness and acceptance

Autism awareness and acceptance are crucial aspects of promoting inclusivity and understanding for individuals on the autism spectrum. By increasing awareness, we can educate the public about the characteristics and needs of individuals with autism, ultimately dispelling misconceptions and stereotypes. Additionally, advocating for acceptance means fostering a society that embraces and supports neurodiversity, recognizing the unique strengths and perspectives that individuals with autism bring to the table.

One of the key reasons why advocating for autism awareness and acceptance is so important is because it can lead to improved support and services for individuals on the spectrum. By raising awareness about autism and its impact on individuals, we can encourage the development of more tailored and inclusive programs that meet the specific needs of those with autism. This can include educational accommodations, employment opportunities, and community resources that promote independence and well-being for individuals with autism.

Furthermore, promoting autism awareness and acceptance can help to reduce stigma and discrimination against individuals with autism. Many people hold misconceptions about autism, viewing it as a deficit or limitation rather than a unique neurodevelopmental trait. By increasing awareness and promoting acceptance, we can challenge these negative attitudes and promote a more inclusive and understanding society. This can create a more welcoming and supportive environment for individuals with autism, allowing them to thrive and contribute to their communities.

Another important aspect of advocating for autism awareness and acceptance is promoting early intervention and support for individuals on the spectrum. Research has shown that early diagnosis and intervention can lead to improved outcomes for individuals with autism, including increased independence and improved social and communication skills. By raising awareness about the importance of early intervention, we can encourage parents, caregivers, and educators to seek help for children who may be showing signs of autism. This can lead to earlier identification and access to support services, ultimately improving the quality of life for individuals with autism.

In addition to improving support and services for individuals with autism, advocating for awareness and acceptance can also lead to greater understanding and empathy among the general population. When people are more informed about autism and its characteristics, they are better able to interact with and support individuals on the spectrum. This can lead to more inclusive and accommodating behavior in schools, workplaces, and communities, creating a more welcoming and supportive environment for individuals with autism. By promoting empathy and understanding, we can foster a society that values and celebrates neurodiversity, recognizing the unique strengths and perspectives that individuals with autism bring to the table. By increasing awareness, challenging misconceptions, and promoting early intervention, we can create a more inclusive and supportive environment for individuals with autism. Additionally, by fostering empathy and understanding, we can promote a society that values and celebrates neurodiversity, recognizing the unique strengths and perspectives that individuals with autism bring to the table. Ultimately, advocating for autism awareness and acceptance is a crucial step towards creating a more inclusive and supportive world for individuals with autism.

Chapter 16: Embracing Neurodiversity

- CELEBRATING INDIVIDUAL differences and strengths

Celebrating individual differences and strengths is essential for creating a diverse and inclusive society. Each person is unique, with their own set of talents, skills, and attributes that contribute to the richness and complexity of our world. By recognizing and valuing these differences, we can foster a culture of respect, understanding, and appreciation for the various ways in which people navigate and experience life.

One of the key benefits of celebrating individual differences and strengths is the promotion of personal growth and self-acceptance. When individuals are encouraged to embrace their unique qualities and talents, they are more likely to develop a sense of confidence and self-worth. This, in turn, can lead to greater motivation and resilience in the face of challenges. By acknowledging and supporting each person's strengths, we can empower them to reach their full potential and achieve their goals.

Moreover, celebrating individual differences and strengths can foster creativity and innovation. When people from diverse backgrounds come together, they bring a wide range of perspectives, ideas, and experiences to the table. This diversity of thought can lead to more effective problem-solving and decision-making, as well as the development of new and innovative solutions to complex problems. By valuing and honoring the unique strengths of each individual, we can create a more dynamic and vibrant community that thrives on collaboration and mutual support.

In addition, celebrating individual differences and strengths can promote a sense of belonging and inclusion. When people feel accepted and valued for who they are, they are more likely to engage fully in their communities and build meaningful relationships with others. This sense of connection can lead to greater social cohesion and a stronger sense of collective identity. By highlighting the diverse strengths and talents of each person, we can create a more inclusive and welcoming environment that embraces the richness of our shared humanity.

It is important to note that celebrating individual differences and strengths does not mean ignoring or minimizing the challenges that people may face. Rather, it involves acknowledging and respecting the experiences and struggles that shape each person's unique perspective and identity. By recognizing the valuable contributions that individuals with diverse backgrounds and abilities bring to the table, we can create a more equitable and just society that values and celebrates the inherent worth and dignity of all its members. By embracing the unique qualities and talents of each person, we can promote personal growth, creativity, innovation, belonging, and inclusion. Through mutual respect and appreciation for the rich tapestry of human experience, we can create a more vibrant and interconnected world that celebrates the beauty and complexity of our shared humanity. Let us continue to celebrate and uplift the individual strengths and differences that make each of us special and unique.

- Promoting acceptance and understanding

Promoting acceptance and understanding in today's increasingly diverse and interconnected world is vital for fostering a more inclusive and harmonious society. In our globalized society, people from different backgrounds, cultures, and beliefs come into contact with one another on a daily basis. This diversity can lead to misunderstandings, stereotypes, and prejudices if not approached with an open mind and a willingness to learn from one another. By promoting acceptance and understanding, we can create a more tolerant and compassionate society where individuals feel valued and respected for who they are.

To promote acceptance and understanding, it is essential to first recognize and acknowledge the diversity that exists within our communities. This means celebrating the unique qualities and experiences that each individual brings to the table, rather than viewing differences as barriers or obstacles. By embracing diversity and fostering an environment of inclusivity, we can create a sense of belonging and acceptance for all members of society, regardless of their background or identity.

One effective way to promote acceptance and understanding is through education and awareness. By educating ourselves and others about different cultures, religions, and perspectives, we can break down stereotypes and misconceptions that may lead to discrimination and prejudice. This can be done through schools, workplaces, and community organizations, where individuals can engage in meaningful conversations and activities that promote empathy and compassion towards others.

Another important aspect of promoting acceptance and understanding is through active listening and empathy. By truly listening to others and trying to understand their viewpoints, we can build connections and bridge divides that may exist between individuals from different backgrounds. By putting ourselves in the shoes of others and striving to see the world through their eyes, we can develop a deeper sense of empathy and understanding that can lead to greater acceptance and mutual respect.

It is also crucial to address and challenge any biases or prejudices that may exist within ourselves and our communities. By confronting our own preconceived notions and prejudices, we can begin to unlearn harmful stereotypes and attitudes that may perpetuate negative behaviors towards others. This requires self-reflection, openness to feedback, and a willingness to engage in difficult conversations that may challenge our beliefs and perspectives.

In promoting acceptance and understanding, it is important to recognize the power of language and communication in shaping our perceptions of others. By using inclusive and respectful language, we can create a more positive and welcoming environment that values diversity and promotes equality. This includes avoiding derogatory language or discriminatory remarks that may harm or marginalize individuals from different backgrounds.

Ultimately, promoting acceptance and understanding requires a commitment to ongoing dialogue, education, and advocacy for social justice and equality. By working together to create a more inclusive and empathetic society, we can build stronger communities that value diversity and promote mutual respect for all individuals. Through our collective efforts, we can create a more accepting and understanding world where differences are celebrated and embraced, rather than feared or judged.

- Embracing the diversity of the autism spectrum

The autism spectrum is a complex and diverse range of neurodevelopmental disorders that affect individuals in various ways. Despite sharing a common diagnostic label, people on the autism spectrum can exhibit a wide array of characteristics, strengths, and challenges. It is essential to recognize and embrace this diversity in order to create a more inclusive and supportive society for individuals with autism.

One of the key aspects of embracing the diversity of the autism spectrum is understanding that no two individuals with autism are alike. Each person on the spectrum is unique, with their own set of strengths, abilities, interests, and challenges. It is important to move beyond stereotypes and assumptions about what autism looks like and instead focus on recognizing and valuing the individual differences that each person brings to the table.

In addition, it is crucial to acknowledge the different ways in which individuals on the autism spectrum may experience the world around them. Some may have difficulty with social communication and interaction, while others may excel in specific areas such as mathematics, music, or art. By recognizing and celebrating these diverse talents and abilities, we can create environments that are more conducive to the success and well-being of individuals with autism.

Another important aspect of embracing the diversity of the autism spectrum is recognizing and supporting the unique needs of individuals on the spectrum. This may involve providing accommodations and modifications in educational and work settings, creating inclusive social and recreational opportunities, and promoting acceptance and understanding within the community. By taking a person-centered approach and listening to the voices of individuals with autism, we can better understand their needs and preferences and provide the support and resources necessary for them to thrive.

It is also essential to acknowledge the intersectionality of autism with other aspects of identity, such as race, gender, sexuality, and culture. Individuals with autism may face additional challenges and barriers due to these intersecting identities, and it is important to address these issues in a holistic and inclusive manner. By recognizing and respecting the diversity of experiences and perspectives within the autism community, we can work towards creating a more equitable and just society for all individuals, regardless of their neurodiversity. By recognizing and celebrating the unique strengths, abilities, and challenges of each person on the spectrum, we can create a more inclusive and supportive environment that values diversity and promotes acceptance and understanding. It is up to all of us to work towards a society where individuals with autism are fully included, respected, and supported in all aspects of life.

Chapter 17: Research and Future Developments

- CURRENT RESEARCH TRENDS and findings

Current research trends and findings in various fields are constantly evolving and shaping the way we understand the world around us. From advancements in technology to breakthroughs in healthcare, researchers are constantly pushing the boundaries of knowledge and innovation in their respective areas of expertise. In this discussion, we will explore some of the latest trends and findings in research across different disciplines, highlighting the impact and implications of these developments.

One of the most significant trends in research today is the increasing focus on interdisciplinary collaboration. Many groundbreaking discoveries are being made at the intersection of different fields, as researchers from diverse backgrounds come together to tackle complex challenges. For example, in the field of artificial intelligence, computer scientists are partnering with biologists to develop new algorithms for analyzing genetic data and improving healthcare outcomes. This collaborative approach has led to a deeper understanding of the underlying mechanisms of disease and has paved the way for personalized medicine.

Another important trend in research is the growing emphasis on data-driven insights and evidence-based decision-making. With the rise of big data and advanced analytics tools, researchers are able to extract valuable information from large datasets and draw meaningful conclusions from their findings. This shift towards data-driven research has revolutionized many fields, from social sciences to environmental studies, enabling researchers to make more informed choices and predictions based on empirical evidence.

In the realm of healthcare, personalized medicine is a key area of research that is gaining momentum. By analyzing an individual's genetic makeup and other biological markers, researchers are able to tailor medical treatments and interventions to the specific needs of each patient. This personalized approach to healthcare has the potential to revolutionize the field, offering more targeted and effective treatments for a wide range of diseases and conditions. As research in personalized medicine continues to advance, we can expect to see significant improvements in patient outcomes and healthcare delivery.

Additionally, research in sustainability and environmental conservation is a burgeoning field that is garnering increasing attention. With the growing awareness of climate change and its impacts on the planet, researchers are exploring new ways to mitigate environmental damage and promote sustainable practices. From developing renewable energy sources to implementing green technologies, researchers are working towards a more sustainable future for generations to come. By studying the complex interactions between human activities and the environment, researchers are able to identify strategies for preserving natural resources and minimizing ecological footprints.

In the realm of social sciences, research on diversity and inclusion is a critical area of investigation that is shaping the way we understand and address social issues. By examining the impact of cultural differences, biases, and inequalities, researchers are able to develop strategies for promoting greater diversity and inclusion in organizations and communities. This research is helping to eliminate barriers to opportunity and create more equitable societies where everyone can thrive. By embracing interdisciplinary collaboration, data-driven insights, personalized approaches, and sustainability practices, researchers are making significant strides towards solving some of the most pressing challenges of our time. As research continues to evolve and expand, we can expect to see even greater advancements in science, technology, healthcare, and social sciences, ultimately improving the quality of life for individuals and communities worldwide.

- Breakthroughs in treatment and interventions

Breakthroughs in treatment and interventions have revolutionized the field of healthcare, offering new hope and possibilities for patients facing a wide range of medical conditions. These advancements are the result of ongoing research, innovation, and collaboration among scientists, healthcare providers, and other professionals in the medical community. By harnessing cutting-edge technology, exploring new treatment modalities, and rethinking traditional approaches to healthcare, breakthroughs in treatment and interventions have the potential to improve patient outcomes, enhance quality of life, and even save lives.

One area that has seen significant breakthroughs in recent years is personalized medicine. This approach to healthcare uses genetic, environmental, and lifestyle factors to tailor treatment plans to individual patients, rather than employing a one-size-fits-all approach. By considering a patient's unique genetic makeup and other relevant factors, healthcare providers can develop more targeted and effective treatment strategies. This personalized approach to medicine has the potential to revolutionize the way we treat a wide range of medical conditions, from cancer to cardiovascular disease to mental health disorders.

Another area of breakthrough in treatment and interventions is the development of precision medicine. Precision medicine is a new approach to healthcare that takes into account individual variability in genes, environment, and lifestyle for each person. This allows doctors and researchers to predict which treatment and prevention strategies will work best for each individual patient. By integrating clinical and molecular data, precision medicine holds promise for improving treatment outcomes and reducing healthcare costs. This approach has been particularly successful in the field of oncology, where targeted therapies have led to improved survival rates and quality of life for cancer patients.

Advances in technology have also played a crucial role in the development of new treatment and intervention strategies. For example, the use of artificial intelligence and machine learning algorithms has enabled researchers to analyze large datasets and uncover hidden patterns and insights that can inform treatment decisions. These computational tools have the potential to revolutionize how we diagnose and treat diseases, allowing for more precise and personalized care. Furthermore, advances in medical imaging, such as MRI and CT scans, have improved our ability to visualize and diagnose medical conditions, leading to more accurate and timely interventions.

In addition to personalized medicine, precision medicine, and technological advancements, breakthroughs in treatment and interventions are also being driven by a better understanding of the underlying mechanisms of disease. Researchers are uncovering new insights into the molecular, genetic, and cellular processes that contribute to the development and progression of various medical conditions. By targeting these underlying mechanisms with novel therapies, researchers are able to develop more effective treatments that may have fewer side effects. This targeted approach to treatment has the potential to transform how we approach healthcare, moving us away from a one-size-fits-all model to one that is more personalized and precise. By harnessing cutting-edge technology, embracing personalized and precision medicine, and understanding the underlying mechanisms of disease, researchers and healthcare providers are developing more effective and targeted treatment strategies. These advancements have the potential to improve patient outcomes, enhance quality of life, and ultimately save lives. As we continue to explore new treatment modalities and refine existing approaches, the future of healthcare looks brighter than ever.

- Looking towards the future of autism support

Autism, a complex neurological condition that affects social interaction, communication, and behavior, has gained increased recognition and understanding in recent years. As awareness of autism has grown, so too has the need for more comprehensive and effective support services for individuals living with autism. Looking towards the future of autism support, it is important to consider the evolving needs of individuals with autism and to develop innovative and person-centered approaches to address those needs.

One of the key challenges in providing support for individuals with autism is the wide range of symptoms and behaviors associated with the condition. Each individual with autism is unique, with their own strengths, challenges, and preferences. As such, it is imperative that support services are tailored to meet the specific needs of each individual. This requires a personalized and holistic approach to care that takes into account the individual's strengths, challenges, interests, and goals. By focusing on the individual as a whole person, rather than just a set of symptoms or behaviors, support services can better meet the needs of individuals with autism and promote their overall well-being and quality of life.

In addition to individualized support, it is also important to consider the role of families and caregivers in the support of individuals with autism. Families and caregivers play a crucial role in supporting individuals with autism, providing them with the love, care, and support they need to thrive. However, caring for a loved one with autism can be challenging and demanding, and caregivers often face significant stress and burnout. Therefore, it is essential to provide support and resources for families and caregivers to help them effectively support their loved ones with autism. This may include access to respite care, counseling, education and training, and other support services to help families and caregivers navigate the challenges of caring for a loved one with autism.

Another important aspect to consider when looking towards the future of autism support is the need for ongoing research and innovation in the field. While much progress has been made in understanding and supporting individuals with autism, there is still much more to learn. By investing in research and innovation, we can continue to improve our understanding of autism and develop new and more effective support services for individuals living with the condition. This may include research into the underlying causes of autism, the development of new interventions and treatments, and the evaluation of existing support services to determine their efficacy and impact.

In addition to individualized support, family support, and research and innovation, it is also important to consider the broader societal context in which individuals with autism live. Individuals with autism often face stigma, discrimination, and barriers to accessing support and services. Addressing these societal and systemic issues is essential to ensuring that individuals with autism are able to fully participate in and contribute to their communities. This may include raising awareness and understanding of autism, promoting inclusion and acceptance, and advocating for policies and practices that support individuals with autism and their families. By addressing these broader societal issues, we can create a more supportive and inclusive environment for individuals with autism to thrive. By focusing on these key areas, we can continue to improve our understanding of autism and develop more effective and inclusive support services for individuals living with the condition. Together, we can create a future where individuals with autism are valued, respected, and supported to reach their full potential.

Chapter 18: Advocacy and Empowerment

- BECOMING AN ADVOCATE for your child

As a parent, it is crucial to understand the importance of advocating for your child in various aspects of their life. Becoming an advocate for your child means being their voice and champion, ensuring that their needs and rights are met in different settings, such as school, healthcare, and social interactions.

One of the key aspects of becoming an advocate for your child is understanding their unique strengths, challenges, and needs. This involves being observant and attentive to your child's behavior, emotions, and interactions with others. By having a clear understanding of your child's individual characteristics, you can better advocate for them in various situations by tailoring your approach and seeking out appropriate resources and services that can address their specific needs.

In the educational setting, becoming an advocate for your child involves actively communicating with teachers, administrators, and other professionals to ensure that your child's academic and social-emotional needs are being met. This may include attending parent-teacher conferences, participating in individualized education plan (IEP) meetings, and collaborating with school staff to develop accommodations and modifications that can support your child's learning.

In the healthcare setting, advocacy for your child involves being proactive in seeking out appropriate medical care, therapies, and interventions that can support their physical and mental health. This may include researching treatment options, consulting with healthcare providers, and advocating for referrals to specialists or therapists who can address your child's specific needs. By actively participating in your child's healthcare decisions and seeking out resources that can benefit their health and well-being, you can ensure that they receive the support and care they need to thrive.

In social situations, advocacy for your child involves fostering positive relationships, promoting social skills development, and supporting their emotional well-being. This may include encouraging your child to engage in social activities, teaching them effective communication and conflict resolution skills, and advocating for inclusive and supportive environments where they can feel accepted and valued. By understanding your child's strengths, challenges, and needs, actively participating in educational and healthcare decisions, and fostering positive social interactions, you can effectively advocate for your child in various settings and ensure that they receive the support and resources they need to thrive. Advocacy is a powerful tool that can empower you as a parent to take an active role in your child's life and advocate for their rights, needs, and well-being in a positive and impactful way.

- Seeking out resources and support

Seeking out resources and support is a crucial part of personal and professional development. Whether you are facing a challenging situation, looking to improve your skills, or simply seeking guidance and encouragement, it is important to know where to turn for help. In this article, we will discuss the importance of seeking out resources and support, as well as provide some tips on how to effectively access and utilize these valuable tools.

One of the key reasons why seeking out resources and support is so important is that no one can succeed on their own. We all face obstacles and challenges in our lives, and having a network of people and resources to rely on can make a huge difference in our ability to overcome these challenges. By reaching out for help when you need it, you can tap into the knowledge, experience, and expertise of others who may have faced similar situations and can provide valuable insights and guidance.

In addition, seeking out resources and support can also help you to expand your own knowledge and skills. Whether you are looking to learn a new skill, gain a deeper understanding of a particular subject, or improve your performance in a certain area, there are countless resources available to help you achieve your goals. From online courses and workshops to mentorship programs and professional organizations, there are endless opportunities to continue growing and learning throughout your life and career.

Furthermore, seeking out resources and support can also provide you with a sense of community and belonging. Knowing that there are people who care about your well-being and are willing to lend a helping hand can be incredibly reassuring and empowering. By building relationships with others who share your interests and values, you can create a supportive network that will stand by you through thick and thin, helping you to navigate the ups and downs of life with confidence and resilience.

So, how can you effectively seek out resources and support to help you achieve your goals and navigate life's challenges. The first step is to identify your needs and goals. What are you struggling with. What skills do you want to develop. What resources do you need to accomplish your objectives. By taking the time to clearly define your goals and needs, you can better target your search for resources and support that will be most beneficial to you.

Once you have identified your needs and goals, the next step is to research and explore the resources and support options available to you. This may involve reaching out to professional organizations, signing up for online courses or workshops, joining a mentorship program, or simply asking for advice from someone you trust. The key is to be proactive and persistent in seeking out the resources and support that will best help you achieve your goals.

In addition to seeking out resources and support, it is also important to be open to asking for help when you need it. Many people struggle with asking for help, seeing it as a sign of weakness or inadequacy. However, seeking support is actually a sign of strength and self-awareness. By being willing to reach out for help when you need it, you can tap into the wisdom and expertise of others, gaining valuable insights and guidance that can help you overcome obstacles and achieve success. By accessing the knowledge, expertise, and support of others, you can overcome challenges, develop new skills, and build a strong support network that will bolster you in your journey through life and career. By being proactive, persistent, and open to asking for help when you need it, you can harness the power of resources and support to achieve your goals and reach your fullest potential. So don't be afraid to reach out for help when you need it - you never know what amazing opportunities and insights may be waiting for you just around the corner.

- Making a positive impact on the autism community

Making a positive impact on the autism community is a crucial endeavor that requires a multifaceted and holistic approach. Autism, a complex neurodevelopmental disorder, affects individuals in different ways and to varying degrees, making it essential to prioritize understanding and support for those affected. By focusing on education, awareness, advocacy, and acceptance, we can create a more inclusive and supportive environment for individuals with autism and their families.

One of the key aspects of making a positive impact on the autism community is education. Educating the public about autism, its challenges, and the strengths and abilities of individuals with autism is essential in dispelling myths and misconceptions. By promoting accurate and up-to-date information about autism, we can increase understanding and empathy, leading to greater acceptance and inclusion. This can be achieved through school-based programs, community workshops, and online resources that provide information and resources for individuals, families, and professionals working with individuals with autism.

In addition to education, awareness plays a crucial role in making a positive impact on the autism community. By raising awareness about autism and its impact on individuals and families, we can work towards reducing stigma and discrimination faced by those with autism. Awareness campaigns, events, and initiatives can help to increase visibility and understanding of autism in society, leading to greater acceptance and support for individuals with autism. By promoting autism awareness, we can create a more inclusive and compassionate community that values the unique contributions of individuals with autism.

Advocacy is another important aspect of making a positive impact on the autism community. Advocacy involves standing up for the rights and needs of individuals with autism, promoting policies and practices that support their well-being and inclusion. By advocating for accessible healthcare, education, employment, and social services for individuals with autism, we can help to create a more equitable and supportive society. Advocacy efforts can range from grassroots activism to policy-level advocacy, with the goal of ensuring that individuals with autism have the resources and support they need to thrive.

Acceptance is also vital in making a positive impact on the autism community. Acceptance involves embracing individuals with autism for who they are, recognizing their unique strengths and challenges, and supporting their autonomy and self-expression. By fostering a culture of acceptance and respect for individuals with autism, we can create a more inclusive and welcoming community that values diversity and celebrates neurodiversity. Acceptance is not just about tolerance, but about actively celebrating and embracing the differences that make each individual unique. By prioritizing understanding and support for individuals with autism, we can create a more inclusive, compassionate, and supportive society that values the contributions of all its members. Through collaborative efforts and a commitment to promoting diversity and inclusion, we can work towards a brighter future for individuals with autism and their families.

Chapter 19: Personal Stories and Reflections

- HEARING FROM PARENTS and individuals with autism

Hearing from parents and individuals with autism is crucial in gaining a better understanding of the unique challenges and strengths of individuals on the autism spectrum. Parents and caregivers play a significant role in the lives of individuals with autism, providing support, advocacy, and resources to ensure their well-being and success. Additionally, individuals with autism are experts on their own experiences and can offer valuable insights into their needs, preferences, and barriers they face in everyday life.

One of the key benefits of hearing from parents and individuals with autism is gaining a better understanding of the diverse range of experiences within the autism community. Autism is a spectrum disorder, meaning that individuals can vary greatly in their abilities, interests, and challenges. By listening to a variety of voices within the autism community, we can better appreciate the individuality of each person with autism and tailor our support and interventions to meet their unique needs.

Parents of individuals with autism can provide valuable insights into the early signs and symptoms of autism, as well as the challenges they face in obtaining a diagnosis and accessing appropriate services. They can also offer perspectives on the impact of autism on family dynamics, relationships, and daily routines. By hearing from parents, practitioners and researchers can gain a more comprehensive understanding of the impact of autism on the family unit and develop strategies to support families in navigating the challenges they face.

In addition to parents, hearing directly from individuals with autism is essential in gaining a deeper understanding of their lived experiences, preferences, and needs. Individuals with autism are often marginalized and their voices overlooked in discussions about their own well-being and future. By actively listening to individuals with autism, we can gain valuable insights into their strengths, interests, and goals, and collaborate with them to develop interventions and supports that are meaningful and effective.

Furthermore, hearing from individuals with autism can help dispel common misconceptions and stereotypes about the autism community. Many people hold mistaken beliefs about autism that can lead to stigma, discrimination, and exclusion. By giving individuals with autism a platform to share their stories and perspectives, we can challenge these misconceptions and promote a more accurate and respectful understanding of autism and neurodiversity. By recognizing and valuing the expertise and perspectives of parents and individuals with autism, we can work together to create a world where all people, regardless of their neurodiversity, have the opportunity to reach their full potential and live fulfilling and meaningful lives.

- Finding inspiration and hope in shared experiences

Finding inspiration and hope in shared experiences is a powerful and transformative aspect of the human experience. When individuals come together to share their stories, struggles, and triumphs, they create a sense of connection and belonging that can be incredibly uplifting and empowering. Whether it is through support groups, online communities, or simply talking with friends and family, sharing experiences with others can provide a sense of comfort and validation that can be difficult to find on one's own.

One of the key benefits of sharing experiences with others is the opportunity to gain perspective and insight that can help individuals navigate their own challenges and obstacles. By listening to the stories of others who have faced similar struggles, individuals can gain a deeper understanding of their own experiences and realize that they are not alone in their journey. This sense of solidarity can be a source of strength and motivation, helping individuals to stay resilient in the face of adversity and maintain a positive outlook even in the darkest of times.

Moreover, sharing experiences with others can also foster a sense of empathy and compassion that can be incredibly healing and transformative.

When individuals open up about their own struggles and vulnerabilities, they create an atmosphere of trust and understanding that allows others to do the same. This reciprocal sharing of experiences can create a sense of mutual support and validation that can be incredibly powerful in fostering a sense of community and connection. By empathizing with the experiences of others, individuals can develop a deeper sense of empathy and compassion that can help them to navigate their own struggles and challenges with greater ease and grace.

In addition to providing comfort and validation, sharing experiences with others can also inspire individuals to take action and make positive changes in their lives. By seeing the resilience and strength of others who have faced similar challenges, individuals can be motivated to make the necessary changes to improve their own circumstances and create a brighter future for themselves. This sense of inspiration and hope can be incredibly empowering, motivating individuals to take control of their own lives and work towards achieving their goals and dreams.

One of the most powerful aspects of sharing experiences with others is the opportunity to build lasting connections and relationships that can provide ongoing support and encouragement. By sharing their stories and experiences with others, individuals can create bonds that can last a lifetime and provide a source of strength and comfort in times of need. These connections can be a source of inspiration and hope, providing individuals with the motivation to keep moving forward and never give up, no matter what challenges they may face. By connecting with others and sharing their stories, individuals can gain perspective, empathy, and inspiration that can help them to navigate their own struggles and challenges with greater ease and grace. As we continue to share our experiences with others, we create a sense of community and connection that can provide ongoing support and encouragement, helping us to stay resilient and hopeful even in the face of adversity. Sharing experiences with others is a powerful reminder that we are all in this together, and by supporting and uplifting one another, we can create a brighter and more hopeful future for ourselves and those around us.

- Reflecting on the journey of raising a child with autism

Raising a child with autism is a unique and complex journey that presents both challenges and rewards. As parents, caregivers, and educators navigate the waters of providing support and understanding for a child with autism, it is important to reflect on the experiences and lessons learned along the way. By taking the time to pause and reflect on the journey of raising a child with autism, individuals can gain insight into their own growth, as well as the growth and development of their child. This reflective process can provide clarity, perspective, and a sense of empowerment in facing the day-to-day struggles and triumphs that come with raising a child with autism.

One of the key aspects of reflecting on the journey of raising a child with autism is recognizing the unique strengths and challenges that each individual with autism possesses. Autism is a spectrum disorder, meaning that it presents differently in each person affected by it. Some children with autism may excel in certain areas, such as math or music, while struggling in others, like social communication or sensory processing. By taking the time to reflect on these strengths and challenges, parents and caregivers can better tailor their support and interventions to meet the specific needs of their child. This personalized approach can help foster a sense of confidence and competence in the child, while also empowering parents and caregivers to advocate for the best possible outcomes for their child.

Another important aspect of reflecting on the journey of raising a child with autism is acknowledging the impact that autism has on the entire family unit. Raising a child with autism can be emotionally, physically, and financially demanding, and it is essential for parents and caregivers to take care of themselves in order to effectively support their child. Reflecting on the impact of autism on the family can help parents identify sources of stress and burnout, as well as strategies for self-care and coping. By prioritizing their own well-being, parents and caregivers can better meet the needs of their child and create a more supportive and nurturing environment for the entire family.

In addition to considering the strengths and challenges of the child with autism and the impact on the family, reflecting on the journey of raising a child with autism also involves celebrating the small victories and milestones along the way. Children with autism may face obstacles in areas such as communication, social interaction, and sensory processing, but they also demonstrate resilience, creativity, and unique perspectives that enrich the lives of those around them. By taking the time to recognize and celebrate these small victories, parents and caregivers can cultivate a sense of gratitude, hope, and joy in their daily interactions with their child. These moments of celebration can help build resilience, strengthen relationships, and foster a sense of community and support for families raising children with autism. By considering the strengths and challenges of the child with autism, acknowledging the impact on the family unit, and celebrating the small victories along the way, individuals can gain a deeper understanding of their own growth and the growth of their child. This reflective process can help parents and caregivers navigate the complexities of raising a child with autism with grace, compassion, and resilience, ultimately creating a supportive and nurturing environment for their child to thrive and succeed.

Chapter 20: Conclusion

- REFLECTIONS ON THE journey of understanding and supporting a child with autism

Understanding and supporting a child with autism can be a challenging journey, but one that is filled with opportunities for growth and learning. Autism spectrum disorder (ASD) is a neurodevelopmental disorder that affects communication, social interaction, and behavior. Each child with autism is unique, with their own strengths and challenges, and it is important to approach each individual with empathy and understanding.

One of the key aspects of supporting a child with autism is understanding their unique communication needs. Many children with autism have difficulty with verbal communication and may rely on nonverbal methods such as gestures, pictures, or devices to communicate their needs and wants. It is important to be patient and attentive when interacting with a child with autism, and to be open to different modes of communication. By taking the time to understand and support their communication needs, you can help them feel understood and valued.

Another important aspect of supporting a child with autism is creating a structured and predictable environment. Children with autism often thrive in environments that are consistent and routine, as it helps them feel safe and secure. By establishing clear routines and expectations, you can help a child with autism feel more comfortable and less anxious. It is also important to provide clear and concise instructions, and to give the child plenty of time to process and respond to information. By creating a structured environment, you can help a child with autism navigate their world more easily and confidently.

In addition to creating a structured environment, it is important to create opportunities for social interaction and peer relationships. Children with autism often struggle with social skills and may find it difficult to connect with their peers. By providing opportunities for social interaction, such as group activities or peer play, you can help a child with autism develop their social skills and build meaningful relationships. It is important to provide support and guidance during social interactions, and to encourage positive social behaviors such as sharing, taking turns, and showing empathy. By fostering social skills and relationships, you can help a child with autism develop important social and emotional skills that will benefit them throughout their lives.

Another important aspect of supporting a child with autism is understanding and addressing their sensory sensitivities. Many children with autism have heightened sensitivities to sensory stimuli such as light, sound, touch, and smell. These sensitivities can be overwhelming and distressing for a child with autism, and may lead to anxiety or meltdowns. It is important to be aware of a child's sensory sensitivities and to create a sensory-friendly environment that minimizes sensory overload. This can include providing a quiet space for the child to retreat to when they are feeling overwhelmed, using sensory tools such as fidget toys or weighted blankets, and being mindful of the sensory triggers that may cause distress. By addressing sensory sensitivities, you can help a child with autism feel more comfortable and regulated in their environment.

In addition to understanding and supporting a child with autism in their daily routines and interactions, it is also important to advocate for their needs and rights. Children with autism may face challenges in accessing education, healthcare, and community resources, and it is important to be their voice and advocate for the support and services they need. This may involve working with educators, healthcare professionals, and community organizations to create individualized plans and accommodations that meet the child's unique needs. By advocating for a child with autism, you can help ensure that they have the support and resources necessary to thrive and reach their full potential. By taking the time to learn about the unique needs and strengths of each individual child with autism, creating a structured and supportive environment, fostering social skills and relationships, addressing sensory sensitivities, and advocating for their needs, you can help a child with autism navigate their world with confidence and success. It is important to approach each child with autism with an open heart and mind, and to celebrate their unique abilities and contributions to the world. By working together as a community to support children with autism, we can create a more inclusive and accepting world where every individual is valued and respected.

- Encouragement for parents to continue advocating and supporting their child

As parents, it is crucial to always advocate for and support your child, no matter their age or circumstances. Your unwavering support can make a significant difference in their overall well-being and success. Advocating for your child means being their voice when they are unable to speak up for themselves, whether it be in school, with healthcare providers, or in social situations. It means standing up for their rights and ensuring that they have access to the resources and opportunities they need to thrive.

Supporting your child goes hand in hand with advocacy. It means being there for them emotionally, mentally, and physically, providing them with the love, care, and guidance they need to navigate life's challenges. Your support can help boost their confidence, self-esteem, and resilience, enabling them to face adversity with strength and determination. As a parent, you are your child's first and most important source of support, and your presence and encouragement can make a world of difference in their lives.

Advocating for your child can sometimes feel daunting, especially when faced with systems and individuals who may not understand or appreciate your child's unique needs. However, it is crucial to remember that you are your child's best advocate and that your efforts can lead to positive outcomes. Whether you are advocating for your child's educational needs, healthcare services, or legal rights, your persistence and determination can help ensure that your child receives the support and accommodations they require to succeed.

One of the most effective ways to advocate for your child is to become well-informed about their specific needs and rights. Educate yourself about the laws, regulations, and policies that govern the services and support available to children and families. Stay up to date on the latest research and best practices in areas related to your child's health, development, and education. By arming yourself with knowledge, you can better advocate for your child and ensure that they receive the services and support they need to thrive.

In addition to being informed, it is essential to communicate effectively with the individuals and organizations involved in your child's care and education. Build positive and constructive relationships with your child's teachers, doctors, therapists, and other service providers, and work collaboratively with them to develop and implement plans that meet your child's needs. Listen to their insights and expertise while also advocating for your child's unique strengths, challenges, and preferences. By working together as a team, you can create a supportive and inclusive environment that fosters your child's growth and development.

It is important to remember that advocating for your child is not a one-time task but an ongoing commitment. As your child grows and changes, their needs and challenges may evolve, requiring you to adjust your advocacy strategies and priorities accordingly. Stay attuned to your child's development and well-being, and be prepared to advocate for their changing needs at every stage of their life. By remaining vigilant and proactive, you can ensure that your child continues to receive the support and resources they need to thrive and succeed. Your advocacy and support can make a lasting impact on your child's well-being, development, and success, helping them navigate life's challenges and reach their full potential. By staying informed, communicating effectively, and remaining committed to your child's needs, you can create a supportive and nurturing environment that empowers your child to thrive. Remember that you are not alone in this journey - there are resources, organizations, and individuals available to support you in your advocacy efforts. Together, we can help ensure that every child receives the care, support, and opportunities they deserve.

- Looking towards a future of acceptance and inclusion for individuals with autism

Individuals with autism spectrum disorder (ASD) face unique challenges in social interactions, communication, and behavior. As our society continues to evolve, it is crucial that we strive towards creating a future that is inclusive and accepting of individuals with autism. By fostering a more understanding and accommodating environment, we can help individuals with autism reach their full potential and lead fulfilling lives.

One of the key factors in promoting acceptance and inclusion for individuals with autism is education. It is important for people to have a basic understanding of what autism is and how it affects individuals. By increasing awareness and knowledge about autism, we can help dispel myths and misconceptions surrounding the disorder. Through education, we can also promote empathy and understanding towards individuals with autism, helping to create a more inclusive society.

In addition to education, it is essential that we advocate for policies and practices that support individuals with autism. This includes providing resources and support services to help individuals with autism navigate daily tasks and challenges. By advocating for the rights of individuals with autism, we can ensure that they have equal access to opportunities and that their voices are heard. Creating a supportive and inclusive environment for individuals with autism requires a collective effort from policymakers, educators, healthcare professionals, and the community at large.

Furthermore, promoting acceptance and inclusion for individuals with autism also involves fostering a supportive and understanding community. This can be achieved by creating opportunities for individuals with autism to engage with others and participate in social activities. By promoting inclusivity in schools, workplaces, and community settings, we can help individuals with autism feel valued and accepted. Building a sense of community and belonging for individuals with autism can have a positive impact on their well-being and overall quality of life.

It is also important to recognize the unique strengths and abilities of individuals with autism. Many individuals with autism have special talents and abilities that can be valuable contributions to society. By focusing on the strengths of individuals with autism and providing opportunities for them to showcase their abilities, we can help build a more inclusive and accepting society. Celebrating the diversity and talents of individuals with autism can also promote a greater sense of understanding and appreciation for their unique perspectives. By increasing awareness, advocating for policies and practices that support individuals with autism, fostering a supportive community, and recognizing the strengths of individuals with autism, we can help build a more inclusive and accepting society. It is important that we continue to work towards creating a world where individuals with autism are valued, respected, and given the opportunity to thrive. Together, we can strive towards a brighter future for individuals with autism.